GUIDE TO CHOOSING, SERVING & ENJOYING WINE

ALLEN R. BALIK

VIRGINIA B. MORRIS

D1371463

LIGHTBULB

PRESS

12/21/03

Dragi Tata,

Živeli !

Voli te tvoji,

Đula i Tena.

Enjoy

LIGHTBULB PRESS
Corporate Staff

Chairman & C.E.O. Kenneth M. Morris
Sales and Marketing Germaine Ma, Karen Meldrom

Project Team

Design Director Dave Wilder
Editorial Staff Karen Lichtenberg, Mavis Morris, Dashiell Robinson
Design Kara W. Hatch
Production Justin V. Bender, Antonina Colbert, Holly Duthie, Christopher Engel, Mercedes Feliciano, Cadence Giersbach, Julie Hair, Gary Lingard, Mike Mulhern, Thomas F. Trojan, Edie Winograde

SPECIAL THANKS

John Livingston, Livingston-Moffett Winery

PICTURE CREDITS

ARCave® (page 133); Barbara Balik (cover, pages 8, 10, 11, 12, 14, 15, 17); Buena Vista Carneros (page 7); Clos Pegase Winery (page 17); Franmara, Inc. (pages 66, 67, 72, 73, 76, 77, 135); Grape Seek, Inc. (pages 30, 31, 32, 33); Kinsale Crystal (page 72); Maximum, Inc. (page 133); Niche Import Co. (page 61); PBC Manufacturing International (page 15)

LIGHTBULB
PRESS

*W*ine is an integral part of my life, my family's life, and the lives of winemakers throughout the United States. Our goal is to be sure that you and other people not only understand our appreciation for wine as a mealtime beverage, but share our belief that it has a positive, civilizing effect on the time you, your family, and friends spend eating and drinking together.

We want you to better appreciate the wines you already know and experiment with new ones. We want you to feel you know enough to approach a wine list with confidence and be comfortable asking for advice from a server, sommelier, or wine retailer. We encourage you to vacation in wine regions in this country and around the world, and put wine tastings on your list of pleasant evening activities.

From the earliest records of our religious traditions and secular cultures, philosophers, statesmen, poets, and scholars have sung the praises of wine. And its popularity keeps growing. Today there are more delicious wines produced around the world than at any time in history, so there's a greater selection in variety and price range. And there's plenty of information in print, on radio and television, and on the Internet if you're interested in learning more about the wines you're drinking.

Few of those resources are more valuable, however, than this handy Guide. It's straightforward, engaging, and down to earth—an ideal introduction if you're new to the pleasures of wine and a handy companion if you're eager to know more.

While the Guide offers lots of practical advice for choosing and serving wine, above all it's meant to share our deep appreciation of the romance, the civilizing effects, and the sheer delight of tasting wine. This is true whether you're having a quiet dinner at home, entertaining friends, or celebrating a special event. To enjoy wine is to partake of a heritage that stretches back to the beginnings of civilization and promises to add continued pleasure to our future.

R. Michael Mondavi
President and CEO
Robert Mondavi

GUIDE TO CHOOSING, SERVING & ENJOYING WINE

THE PLEASURES OF WINE

DEMYSTIFYING WINE

IT'S ALL IN THE DETAILS

TABLE OF CONTENTS

*D*INING OUT

*E*NTERTAINING AT HOME

*C*OLLECTING AND TASTING

A Brief History of Wine

Viticulture has been part of human culture for thousands of years.

Like so many other important innovations, wine was probably discovered by accident. You can imagine the surprise and the delight of your ancient ancestors as they took a sip of what they expected to be grape juice—only to discover the delicious flavors and delightful effects of the strangely altered brew.

Explorers spread viticulture around the world.

Egyptian winemakers at work and the wine cellar in the pyramid at Sakkara.

1500 BC   600 BC

ON THE RECORD

There's no way to pinpoint the date or the circumstances of that first taste of wine, or to discover much about its use in prehistoric times. But there's persuasive visual and written evidence about wine's prominent place in ancient civilizations, dating back to at least 3000 BC. Among the oldest are a scene depicting wine bearers in a carved panel uncovered in the Mesopotamian civilization of Ur, a Biblical reference to Noah planting a vineyard in the Caucasus mountains after he emerged from the Ark, and detailed inscriptions on the amphorae, or wine jugs, found in Egyptian tombs.

More recent tombs, dating to about 1500 BC, are decorated with wall paintings and reliefs that depict in explicit detail how grapes were grown, harvested, and crushed, as well as the vats where the juice was fermented. In his epic tales of the fall of Troy and the journeys of Odysseus composed around 1000 BC, Homer describes the seas as wine-dark, and depicts his characters drinking wine in a number of episodes.

TRAVELING VINES

As the Greeks colonized Sicily, southern Italy, and southern France, they took their vine cuttings, winemaking techniques, and wine drinking traditions with them. And in northern Italy, particularly in Tuscany, which is still a major wine region, wines were being produced both from native vines and those imported from Asia.

As the Roman Empire expanded through western Europe, vineyards were cultivated in Bordeaux and Burgundy, the Rhone and Rhine Valleys, the Iberian peninsula, and as far north as southern England.

There are more than 2,000 operating wineries in the US, in 48 of the 50 states. Alaska and North Dakota are the exceptions.

THE PLEASURES OF WINE

WINE IN THE US

By worldwide standards, winemaking has a very, very short history in the US. But native grapes were so abundant on the east coast when explorer Leif Ericson arrived about 1000 AD that he called his discovery Vinland.

French and Spanish explorers brought grapevines with them from Europe, and settlers cultivated native vines to make Catawba and other distinctly American wines. French Huguenot settlers were making wine in Florida in the 1600s, and Thomas Jefferson planted a vineyard in Virginia in the 1700s.

In California, Spanish missionaries grew grapes to make sacramental wine for their congregations. As missions spread throughout the state, so did the vineyards. Though the mission grape is nearly extinct today—a few tiny vineyards in southern California produce minuscule quantities—other grapes are thriving. By the 1830s, winemaking was no longer the domain of the church, and by century's end nearly a dozen major wineries had been established, including some that are still in operation: Beringer, Korbel, Simi, and Wente.

Agoston Haraszthy, who founded Buena Vista Winery in 1857, on 560 acres near the town of Sonoma, was one of the most influential and flamboyant figures in California wine history. He's credited with

Agoston Haraszthy

bringing premium European grape varieties—100,000 cuttings of 300 different vines—back to California in 1861 and making the first zinfandel. While he didn't stick around to see it flourish—legend has it he was consumed by an alligator in Nicaragua—he ushered in a new era in US winemaking.

AND A DRY SPELL

Prohibition, which lasted from 1919 to 1933, almost wiped out the US wine industry. Some producers survived by making sacramental wine for religious institutions. But prized vineyards were largely abandoned, and unused wineries fell into disrepair.

Ironically, grape production increased. That's because although the sale of alcoholic beverages was banned, it was legal for people to produce wine if they were going to drink it themselves.

But these home winemakers needed grapes that could be stored longer and survive shipping better than the varieties professional winemakers preferred. To meet that demand, growers planted heartier varieties, including alicante bouschet and zinfandel. Zinfandel, in particular, remains a popular favorite—perhaps the one positive consequence of that dry period.

200 AD

1857 AD

Votive stele showing a Carthaginian viticultural scene. From 800 BC until it was destroyed by the Romans, winemaking flourished in Carthage.

$\mathcal{F}$ruit of the Vine

Geography and weather are major players in making wine.

You can find grapevines growing almost everywhere—along hiking trails, at the beach, maybe in your backyard. But great wines are made from very particular vines planted in very particular places.

Virtually all fine wine grapes—there's a huge variety of them—belong to a single genus and species, *Vitis vinifera*. And the vineyards in which they thrive are in temperate zones, with rainy, cold but not frigid winters, and long, fairly hot summers. Ideal wine regions are found in Europe, California and several other US states, Australia and New Zealand, South Africa, Chile, and other South American countries.

LOCATION, LOCATION

Grape quality—and the quality of the wine that can be produced from the grapes—depends first and foremost on the vineyard where the vines are planted. *Terroir*, a French word without an exact English translation, is the sum total of the vineyard's soil and subsoil, including tiny quantities of minerals, the rainfall, drainage, sun exposure, and other physical factors. In regions of California, for example, it includes the fog that rolls in regularly off the Pacific. The closest you can come to the concept in English is to think of *terroir* as the grapevine's environment.

CLIMATE CONTROL

Not every wine grower wants to plant in the same climate. Those who mass-produce wine prefer warmer areas where vines flourish and grape yields are large. Growers focused primarily on making premium wines prefer less fertile soils and somewhat cooler areas, especially those where temperatures rise during the day and cool off significantly at night.

That's why many of the great vineyards of the world are located near bodies of water—seas, rivers, and lakes—or mountain passes. In that geography, a day/night differential of 30° to 50° Fahrenheit is not unusual.

WINE IS MADE ON FIVE CONTINENTS

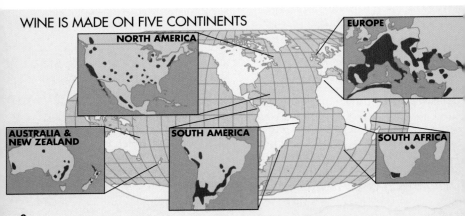

EUROPE

NORTH AMERICA

AUSTRALIA & NEW ZEALAND

SOUTH AMERICA

SOUTH AFRICA

> **"** For me, the most exciting aspect of what I do is discovering how character, intensity, and quality can vary with each site. With a great site, the role of the vintner is that of guide, not maker. **"**
>
> —*Paul Draper*
> *Ridge Vineyards*

To make things more complicated, vineyards are usually located in areas that have a number of microclimates. From a wine grower's perspective these are small pockets of land with different sun exposures and breezes. As a result, weather conditions can vary tremendously over the next hill or even from one adjacent vineyard to another. That helps to explain why different grape varieties, which may require very different growing conditions, can be grown successfully in relatively close proximity, and how the same variety can produce wines of different character.

A CHANGE IN THE WEATHER

Wine growers, like other farmers, are never completely satisfied with the weather. That's because even seemingly modest variations can make a huge difference in the year-to-year quality of a vineyard's crop.

A little too much or not enough rain, frost coming too late in the spring, hail or strong winds just at the wrong time can diminish or destroy the crop and sometimes damage the vines as well.

Timing is everything. For example, a heavy rain late in the growing season may make the grapes swell and dilute their juice, or promote the growth of harmful molds that make the grapes rot. Hot, sunny days are perfect for drying up the rain and preventing mold. But, late in the season, there are fewer hot days and a greater threat of rain.

AGE BEFORE BOUNTY

Vines typically start producing usable grapes about three years after planting. They continue to mature for another four to seven years, yielding more and better grapes, provided growing conditions are right. The average productive life of quality winemaking vines is about 30 to 40 years. But some old vines, including zinfandel, can go on producing quality grapes for 100 years or more.

Long-established vineyards have regular replanting programs in place, so that they always have vines in full production. But sometimes growers must rip out and replant their vineyards if the vines have been damaged by weather or stricken by disease.

VINTAGE WEATHER

Vintage—which is the year in which a particular grape crop is harvested—often gets lots of attention when people are talking about wine. Usually, the question being debated is whether one vintage is better than another. Is that a real concern?

The answer is yes. Weather has a major impact on grape quality, and weather varies from year to year. Increasingly, winemakers using sophisticated winemaking equipment can minimize the effects of these variations, but they can't eliminate them altogether. Vintage may be especially important in wines that typically get better as they get older, since the factors that affect wine as it ages—its acid, fruit, and tannin levels—are directly influenced by weather.

On the other hand, most wines are consistent enough from year to year that it takes an expert to identify a particular vintage. Even if the same winery produces a radically different wine in one year, different isn't necessarily bad. In fact, since tastes are personal, you may prefer a wine from a year that's described as a less-than-ideal vintage.

> **"** We choose vineyard sites primarily based on location in a proven appellation. Then we go to the specific terroir. But none of the physical characteristics matter unless the winegrower captures their attributes and makes the best possible varietal wine. **"**
>
> —*Dan Duckhorn*
> *Duckhorn Vineyards*

A Vineyard Year

Life in the vineyard has a seasonal rhythm.

Though no two vineyards are exactly alike, all vineyards go through the same natural cycle of rest, new growth, development, and harvest every year.

WINTER

Sap flows downward towards the roots as the vines slip into hibernation. They are quiet, but alive, standing like statues, leafless, their russet canes a sign of the season just finished. This is the time for wine growers to pause, reflect, review the season past, and plan the season ahead. There are some tough questions:

Were their vines balanced, leaf canopy to fruit load?

How do they prune for the best wine quality?

How can they improve the overall vineyard operations next year?

What are their reactions, and the winemakers', to the new wine? What will it be like, in flavor, style, and alcoholic content?

SPRING

A glorious time! Vines are being reborn. Sap begins to flow upward. Days are warming. Buds swell, popcorn fuzz peeks out, and tiny iridescent green leaves and stems stretch forth. These fragile shoots are vulnerable and need protection. They are tender and tasty to rabbits, deer, and insects, perfect for mildew, and can be blackened by frost. Wine growers are guardians and guides during these critical times.

By May, shoot strength comes, but with it a new vulnerability. Flower clusters appear, again tiny, without petals, only the white pollen showing. With fingers crossed, eyes to the sky, winemakers wait for pollination to begin. Fertilization occurs: early for chardonnay and pinot noir, later for cabernet, syrah, and zinfandel.

THE TIMING OF HARVEST

Every year, growers and winemakers agonize about the best time to harvest the crop. Pick too early, and the grapes won't have had enough time to reach their peak. Pick too late, and the grapes could be overripe. Worse, the crop could be battered by a rain storm or lost to an early autumn freeze.

Judging the right degree of ripeness is crucial to winemaking. As grapes get ripe, their acidity drops and their sugar content increases. Grapes used to make crisp white wines, such as sauvignon blanc or reisling, are picked earlier than grapes used for sweeter dessert wines.

SUMMER

The first signs of summer are the berries: first the size of peppercorns, then the size of peas. Days are long and warm, nights are cool. Temperatures spiral to 90° and sink to 50° Fahrenheit. Mid-season is marked by *veraision:* the softening of the white grape skins and the coloring of the red grape skins. Seeds begin to mature. Ripening is in full swing!

Growers monitor the vines for stress, water judiciously, keep them on the edge, and wait patiently. Fall is approaching. They remove some leaves to allow dappled sunlight to mature the remaining fruit. Fruit is thinned to concentrate flavor intensity in the remaining clusters.

BRIX, NOT MORTAR

As grapes ripen, US wine growers measure **brix**, or the percentage of sugar by weight in their juice, using a device called a refractometer. Brix is one important indicator of when to harvest because the sugar level, which increases as the grapes get riper, determines a wine's ultimate alcohol content. (In fact, in Europe, the percentage of sugar is called degrees of potential alcohol.)

Similarly, the tannins that give some red wines their distinctive characteristics increase and mature as the grapes ripen. So, red-wine grapes such as zinfandel and cabernet sauvignon are picked later than most white-wine grapes. The color of the skins gets richer, as well, and the aromas change—both of which affect the finished product.

TIMING IS ALL

If you're making quality wine, speed is critical once the grapes are picked. They can be damaged easily and deteriorate quickly. So the goal is to move the harvest from the vineyard to the winery as fast as possible, keeping the fruit cool before crushing.

FALL

Harvest is near! Expectations are high! All of the efforts of the year culminate at the ultimate moment when the picker's knife severs the precious cluster from the mother vine. There is no turning back, no tomorrow. Winemakers are like expectant parents, full of anticipation and questions:

When is the ultimate moment?

Is it driven by art or science, or both?

Is the fruit ripe by the numbers or fully mature and full of flavor?

How are the acid and the pH doing?

What about the weather?

Will there be more sun or is the first rain just off the coast?

With most of the questions answered, the harvest begins and fermentations start to bubble. When the harvest is complete, the winemakers, exhausted and hopeful that the wines are worthy of greatness, relax and catch their breath—just in time to have a bite of turkey from their Thanksgiving table.

A Vineyard Year text by
Randle Johnson
The Hess Collection Winery

Winemaking

Winemaking is a balance of tradition and technology.

At one level, all winemaking is alike. But every winemaker has his or her own goals and techniques. Differences in timing the harvest or handling the grapes, which might seem insignificant to an outsider, have a major impact on the character of the wine he or she produces.

So does each choice that's made at every step in the process of making grapes into wine. The last decision is when it's time to release the vintage, which can be in a matter of days, or not for years.

CRUSHING AND PRESSING

Once upon a time, barefoot and often naked men, women, and children really did dance in vats of freshly-picked grapes. But in most of the world, they've been replaced by other, admittedly less colorful, specialized pieces of machinery that crush or press the grapes, releasing their juice without breaking their bitter seeds. Some winemakers crush, some press, and some use both methods.

Despite the impression that the words crush and press may give, the machines

Red Grapes are crushed before fermentation and pressed after

CRUSHER

White Grapes are crushed and pressed before fermentation

PRESS

are, in fact, extremely gentle on the fruit. In a crusher, the ripe, soft grapes are pushed through paddles or rollers to break their skins. The juice, seeds, and skin, a mixture that is known as the **must**, slip through openings in a revolving drum inside the crusher and collect at the bottom.

There are several types of wine presses, each of which handles the task somewhat differently. But the basic operating principle is the same: Grapes are gently pushed against a fixed object to release their juice. Winemakers producing high-quality wine carefully control the pressure they use on the grapes to prevent breaking the seeds and making the juice bitter. Winemakers who want the greatest possible yield can use added pressure to extract as much juice as possible.

> My passion to make the best wine in the world got me involved in winemaking. Feedback from around the world confirming I'm succeeding is my greatest reward.
>
> —*Jayson Pahlmeyer*
> *Pahlmeyer*

CRUSHING STATISTICS
A ton of grapes yields between 60 and 70 cases of wine, or 720 to 840 bottles.

FERMENTATION

Fermentation is the magical process that turns grape juice into wine. Yeasts are the tiny organisms that make it happen.

Strictly speaking, fermentation occurs when either natural yeast or yeast that has been inoculated into the must converts sugar in the grape juice into alcohol, specifically ethanol, and carbon dioxide (which vents off, or escapes into the air). And while it's a natural process, the best winemakers coddle their product along every step of the way.

White wines are fermented without their skins in stainless steel vats or tanks, or in wooden, typically oak, barrels, depending on the end result the winemaker wants.

As the fermentation progresses, the yeast cells die and drop to the bottom of the container, forming what are known as lees. Then the wine is either drawn off, a process known as racking, or allowed to age in contact with the lees, or *sur lie*. That's also the winemaker's choice, and depends on the bouquet and flavors he or she wants in the finished product.

BUBBLE, BUBBLE

Although some winemakers use only the natural, or wild, yeast that grows on grape skins, most add cultured commercial yeast to the must to start the fermentation process. A variety of yeasts is available, and winemakers choose particular ones not only to assure a more complete, consistent fermentation at the speed they choose, but also to produce particular flavors and aromas in the wine.

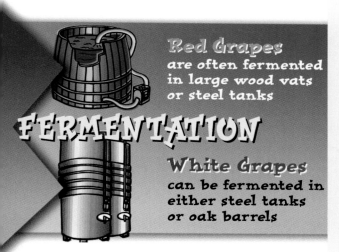

Red Grapes are often fermented in large wood vats or steel tanks

FERMENTATION

White Grapes can be fermented in either steel tanks or oak barrels

COLORING WINE

Virtually all wine is made from white juice, but it is treated differently during fermentation of red, white, and rosé wines.

For white wine, juice is separated immediately from the must and transferred to a barrel or tank before fermentation begins.

For red wine, the juice and skins are left together so that the wine's distinctive color is extracted from, or drawn out of, the color of the skins.

To make a rosé, the winemaker either leaves the juice on the grape skins for a limited period to produce the wine's distinctive color, or blends a small amount of red wine into white wine.

SEEING RED

Red wines can present a greater winemaking challenge than whites, since the process involves not only converting sugar to alcohol but simultaneously extracting color and tannin from the skins. Ideally, the greatest possible surface area of the juice must be in contact with the skins throughout the process to produce the results the winemaker is aiming for.

However, the skins tend, inconveniently, to clump together and rise to the top of the tank, forming what's known as a cap that floats on the surface of the juice. Winemakers deal with the **cap** in one of two ways, based on their own experience or preference. They either pump the juice gently over the cap, whether constantly or periodically, so the color and tannin drain down through the juice, or periodically punch the cap down into the juice, either manually or mechanically. Both methods get the job done.

The Finishing Touches

Making wine is a combination of art and science.

After fermentation, most red wines, and some whites, go through a secondary, bacterial fermentation known as malolactic fermentation.

Bacteria, which may be either naturally present in the juice or inoculated into it, convert the malic acid which is present in the grape juice and has distinctive green apple flavors into lactic acid, which has soft, creamy, and buttery flavors. The end result is a wine with a milder, less acidic taste, and, in certain cases, greater complexity.

Racking is the least invasive approach to clarification. The particles are allowed to settle to the bottom of the tank or barrel, and the wine is drawn off. Most wines undergo several rounds of racking before they're bottled.

Fining is another way to clarify a cloudy wine. Winemakers add a fining agent, such as egg whites or a clay known as bentonite, which attracts floating particles and pulls them to the bottom of the container. Again, the clear wine is drawn off, and the sediment is left behind.

Both red and white wines can be aged in traditional oak barrels or stainless steel tanks

AGING

A winemaker can simply let the process happen, can make it happen, or can actively prevent it, either in an entire production or in a certain percentage of it. The decision is driven by the aromas and flavors the winemaker wants in the finished wine.

WHEN FERMENTATION'S DONE

After fermentation, many wines contain floating particles, including yeast cells, clumped tannins, and protein particles, that make the wine look cloudy. So, many winemakers use one or more standard techniques to clarify their wines.

AGING

Some wines, including Beaujolais nouveau, are ready to drink as soon as fermentation ends. Most others benefit from aging, a process of slow oxidation that allows their flavors and bouquets to mature and become more complex.

Wine can be aged in a traditional wooden barrel, a larger wooden oval, or a stainless steel tank. An entire lot can be aged the same way, or parts of it in different ways. For example, a winemaker might age some wine from a lot in new oak barrels and some in older oak barrels, and blend the two lots together before bottling.

> We have a good idea of what an ideal vintage should be for a particular growing area and particular wine style. When less than desirable vintages come along, we can adjust vineyard and winemaking practices to partially compensate.
>
> —*Joe Cafaro*
> *Cafaro Cellars*

The choice of wood or stainless steel depends on the type of wine that's being made and the winemaker's style, which defines the characteristics he or she wants the wine to have. If the goal is a fresh and lively white wine, it won't be aged very long before bot-

vanilla, and butter-scotch flavors that are popular with some consumers more cheaply, certain producers add oak chips or shavings to the wine after fermentation and filter them out before bottling.

BOTTLING

Since most bottling is done from tanks, not individual barrels, wines that have been aged in barrels are mixed together, or blended, in large tanks and allowed to settle. After settling, wines may be drawn directly into the bottle or fined (by the addition of egg white or bentonite) and/or filtered to produce what appears to be a cleaner and clearer wine.

Some white wines are chilled before bottling to encourage the precipitation, or settling out, of

Barrel-aged wine is mixed a final time in tanks before bottling

BOTTLING

Some white wines are chilled in tanks before bottling

tling. And it will rarely, if ever, be aged in oak, which adds its own distinctive flavors and seasonings.

In contrast, some whites and many reds are aged in oak for a longer time before bottling because the winemaker wants more development and complexity added to the natural flavors of the grape.

Since oak barrels are very expensive, and barrel aging can be a long, time-consuming process, some wines aren't aged in oak. To get the oak,

potassium tartrate, a salt crystal that occurs naturally in the wine. This process, known as cold stabilization, is used to prevent crystals from forming later in the bottle. If you do see crystals from time to time—usually on the bottom of the cork or in the bottom of your glass—don't be concerned. They're completely tasteless, absolutely harmless, and cause no problems.

Wine People

Making wine means wearing many hats—from farmer to scientist to marketer.

Are you uncertain about the difference between a wine grower and a winemaker, a vintner and a viticulturist, or about what a wine producer is?

Part of the confusion is that the terms sound similar, and are often used interchangeably. A wine grower, also producer may encompass the wide-ranging responsibilities and varied skills involved in growing grapes, turning them into wine, and marketing the wine successfully. In that sense, a producer is a person who wears many different hats.

Wine Producer

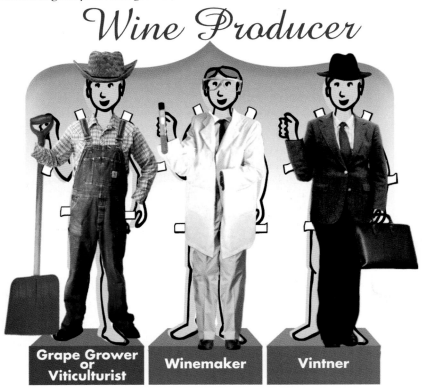

Grape Grower or Viticulturist — **Winemaker** — **Vintner**

called a viticulturist, plants vines, cultivates vineyards, and harvests grapes. A winemaker is responsible for fermenting, aging, blending, and bottling the wine. A producer may be the grower, a family-controlled company that owns the land where the grapes are grown, the winery where the wine is made, or a large corporation. A vintner is a another term for a winery owner or winemaker.

Sometimes the distinctions between these roles are clearly maintained, and sometimes they're intertwined. For example, the job of the

WHO DOES WHAT

In a large wine-producing operation that turns out millions of bottles each year, there's often very little contact between grower and winemaker, or, more precisely, between the many growers whose grapes the company buys and the many winemakers in charge of the different wines the company makes.

That's not the case in smaller, often grower-owned operations. There, the wine grower and the winemaker—who may be the owner, a partner, a full-time employee, or an independent consultant who works for several

> 🍷🍷 I know of no other business that's more fun or more stimulating than wine. Doing it as a family is roughly perfect. 🍷🍷
>
> —*John Livingston*
> *Livingston-Moffett Winery*

different wineries—must work closely and compatibly together to produce the style and quality of wine they're jointly striving to create.

A different situation exists when wineries don't own their own vineyards. They establish relationships, often long-term ones, with growers to buy the grapes they need to produce and sell wine under their own or a proprietary name. Or, growers may take their grapes to a winery that has the room to handle additional production and pay a fee for having their wines produced.

Finally, growers may belong to a **cooperative**, a jointly owned winery, where they take their grapes to be fermented and aged, and then bottled to be sold under their individual names.

A MATTER OF STYLE

Two accomplished winemakers, starting with grapes from the same vineyard, are likely to produce wines that are distinctly different. While experts may not agree on which of the two is the more pleasing wine, they would agree that the differences are the result of two factors: the winemaker's skill and sense of style.

A winemaker may influence what a wine will be like by deciding:

- How long and at what temperature to ferment the juice
- How long to age the wine, and in what kind of container
- When and how often to rack
- Whether to blend juice that has gone through malolactic fermentation with juice that has not, or whether to blend juice from grapes grown in different vineyards
- When to bottle the wine
- When to release the wine for sale

A SENSE OF PLACE

While you could call the property where wine grapes are grown a farm, you're more apt to hear it described as a vineyard, a winery, or an estate.

VINEYARD

A vineyard is specifically a plot of land where grapes are grown. When a vineyard consistently produces distinctive, high-quality grapes, the wines made

from those grapes may carry the vineyard's name. In the US, some vineyard names are so closely associated with a wine that no varietal name is used to identify it.

WINERY

A winery is a place where winemaking takes place, often a building or buildings and the surrounding grounds. It may also be the place where wines are aged and bottled. Ideally, a winery is close to the vineyards where the grapes are grown, since the faster the fermentation process begins, the smaller the opportunity for the grapes to spoil.

Estate

When a US wine is labeled "estate bottled," all of the grapes were grown on land owned or controlled by a specific winery located within a specific viticultural area (AVA).

In addition, the wine was crushed, fermented, aged, and bottled at the winery (or at a cooperative to which the winery belongs). Similar rules apply in other countries.

Sparklers

Some winemakers march to a different drummer.

No wines are more romantic and festive than the fine sparkling wines made in the French region of Champagne and elsewhere in the world.

Traditionally, fine sparkling wines are made following the process known as the **_méthode champenoise_**, developed by the Benedictine monk Dom Perignon in the 17th century. In simple terms, the process involves blending still wines, fermenting the mixture a second time in the bottle, and then removing the wine from the sediment that accumulates during that fermentation.

The distinctive bubbles of sparkling wines are created by carbon dioxide that's produced during the second fermentation and trapped in the bottle. The unique flavors and styles of these wines are the result of the art and skill of the individual winemakers.

> The winemaking behind premium sparkling wine, the art of blending in particular, is a bit underappreciated. Because the still wines we start with are made from less ripe fruit than the fruit used for table wines, their individual characters are less intense. So we must blend many individual wines to come up with a final product that will please and resonate.
>
> —*Hugh Davies*
> *Schramsberg*

THE RIDDLER AT WORK

Although there are machines that can handle remuage, much sparkling wine is still riddled manually. The accomplished riddler will precisely rotate and tilt from 20,000 to 30,000 bottles a day. By general agreement, the job is one of most skilled in the entire wine industry.

THE RIDDLE OF SPARKLING WINES

To make sparkling wine, the winemaker blends still wines that may come from different vintages, grape varieties, and vineyards to create a particular style of wine—sometimes described as house style—that's consistent from year to year. That blend is stored in neutral containers until it is ready to be bottled for the second fermentation.

To start the second fermentation, the winemaker adds to each bottle a precise amount of sugar in solution with some wine and fresh yeast. The bottle is stoppered, usually with a metal cap, and laid on its side. As this fermentation progresses, usually over a period of one to three months, dead yeast cells, or lees, drop to the inside wall of the bottle as sediment.

When the winemaker determines the time is right, the process of *remuage* is begun. During *remuage,* bottles are placed in special racks, cap down, at about a 45° angle. Each day for about a month, the *remueur,* more commonly called the riddler, rotates each bottle a precise amount and tilts it at a slightly greater angle. This process continues until the bottle is vertical and the sediment has moved completely into the neck and rests against the cap.

When *remuage* is completed, the sediment that has collected at the cap of the vertical bottle is **disgorged**, a tricky and delicate process that must be handled quickly. Not only must the sediment be removed, but the sweetness of the wine must be adjusted, and the bottle must be corked to withstand the tremendous internal pressure in the bottle—about six atmospheres, or 90 pounds of pressure per square inch.

OUT WITH THE SEDIMENT

To remove the sediment, the neck of the bottle is immersed in an icy brine or other solution which instantly freezes a small amount of wine at the cap, trapping the sediment. The bottle is quickly uprighted and the cap removed. The pressure in the bottle, which developed during the second fermentation, discharges, or disgorges, the frozen plug holding the sediment from the bottle.

The small amount of wine which froze around the sediment is replaced by topping off the bottle with the *Liqueur d'Expedition*—a solution of wine and sugar also referred to as **doseage**. The doseage also adjusts and fixes the level of sweetness to balance the natural acidity of the wine. The cork and wire basket are then put in place and the bottled wine is again laid on its side until it is labeled and released for sale.

OTHER WAYS TO BUBBLE

To speed up the time-consuming process, and usually to reduce the cost, sparkling wine is also made in non-traditional ways. But putting "bottle fermented" on the label doesn't mean the same thing as "*méthode champenoise*" or "fermented in this bottle." What it means is that the wine may have been made by the transfer method: fermented in one bottle, moved to a vat, filtered, and transferred, under pressure, to another bottle.

Sparkling wine can also be fermented the second time in tanks, filtered, and bottled under pressure. In most cases, this method makes inexpensive blends into inexpensive sparkling wines. Cheaper yet, some sparkling wines are made by adding carbon dioxide to still wine, in much the same way soda gets its fizz.

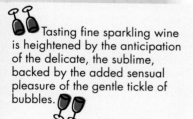

Tasting fine sparkling wine is heightened by the anticipation of the delicate, the sublime, backed by the added sensual pleasure of the gentle tickle of bubbles.

—*Eileen G. Crane*
Domaine Carneros Ltd.

A MATTER OF TASTE

There are six different ways to describe sparkling wine, ranging from most dry to most sweet.

DRY

Naturale
Extra brut
Brut
Extra sec or Extra dry
Sec or dry
Demi-sec

SWEET

The irony is that, while sec means dry, it really describes various degrees of sweetness.

Other Wines, Other Tastes

There are lots of delicious reasons to expand your wine horizons.

The still and sparkling wines you drink before or during dinner, or use to celebrate a special occasion, may be the wines you know best. But they're not the whole story. There's a world of other wines—some sweet and some dry, some fortified and others distilled—that you'll also want to explore.

WHAT'S FOR DESSERT?

Some of the greatest wines in the world are the dessert wines made from riesling, chenin blanc, or a blend of sémillon and sauvignon blanc grapes, among others. The grapes are left on the vine beyond the normal end of the harvest, sometimes until they're so dehydrated they begin to resemble raisins. As time goes by, the grape sugars get more concentrated, and the flavors get more intense.

By the time the grapes are picked, the sugar levels may be twice what they are in grapes used for table wine, which means not all of the sugar is converted to alcohol during fermentation. The residual sugar that remains after the fermentation stops makes the wines naturally sweet. This sweetness, however, is balanced by the naturally occurring high acidity of these grapes, so the wines should not be cloying.

Grapes with noble rot

I had a dream when I first came to California, of creating a brandy capable of maintaining the intensity and brightness of the fruit, even after many years of aging, by distilling and blending many different premium grapes.

—*Hubert Germain-Robin*
Germain-Robin

In some cases, the grapes develop a fuzzy, blue-gray mold, known as noble rot, that's caused by the *Botrytis cinerera* fungus. The fungus pierces holes in the grape's skin, allowing moisture to escape, further concentrating the sugars and flavors. Botrytised grapes have unique and complex layers of flavor that mesh with and intensify the natural sweetness of the wines that are made from them.

IN THE GLASS

Dessert wines are more intense than table wines, both in appearance and flavor, and a little can go a long way. Typically, you can serve six to eight people with a half bottle, the size in which many of these wines are sold.

You can serve the wine in any glass, including those you normally use to serve table wine. But some people prefer the smaller size that's often used to serve sherry or port. Unlike those fortified wines, which are usually served at room temperature, you may want to

Apéritif	Dessert wine (Digestif)
Ratafia	Port
Lillet	Grappa
Vermouth	Late Harvest Wines
Kir	Marc
Madeira	Sherry

20

serve dessert wines at the same temperature or slightly cooler than you would serve a typical white wine. This helps intensify the acid and better balance the sweetness.

A FROZEN TREAT

Eiswein is one of the rarest, and for some people, the most delicious, of all dessert wines. It's made from very ripe riesling grapes that are on the vine until the first frost. The frozen grapes are picked before dawn and pressed immediately, and the juice is fermented into a naturally sweet, intensely flavored wine.

Since eiswein can be made only when conditions are right, and those times can't be reliably predicted, some producers use grapes they have frozen in cryogenic rooms rather than on the vine. Opinion is mixed on the results: Some people claim you can't tell the difference between eiswein and its imitators. Others insist there is simply no comparison.

FORTIFIED WINES

Fortified wines may be served as aperitifs before a meal, with certain foods during the meal, or at the end of the meal, with coffee. These wines are similar in that they're created when a winemaker adds a distilled wine, or brandy, without distinctive aromas or flavors, to a wine. But each fortified wine is also distinctive, depending on the style of the original wine, the amount of brandy that's added to it, and the point at which that addition is made.

Port, for example, is fortified early, which means the brandy is added while fermentation is still going on. That not only increases the alcohol level but stops the fermentation and leaves unfermented residual sugar.

Sherries, in contrast, are usually fortified late, after fermentation has ended. That helps to explain why they are often dry rather than sweet. Dulce, a concentrated wine, is often added to adjust the sweetness.

Some fortified wines, like vermouth and Dubonnet, get their distinctive flavors and aromas from flavor compounds, such as wormwood (in the case of vermouth), herbs, spices, and vanilla, that are added to the liquid.

THE HARD STUFF

Wine can also be distilled into brandy. The process involves boiling the wine, collecting the alcohol steam that evaporates, and condensing the steam into a concentrated (and intense) liquid. The most highly regarded brandies are produced in a pot-still, or alembic, by skilled distillers. Others are distilled, more inexpensively, in what's known as a continuous still.

HAVE SOME MADEIRA, MY DEAR

Madeira, from the island of the same name off the coast of western Africa, is also a fortified wine. But it didn't start out that way.

In the colonial period, barrels of conventional wine were shipped regularly to the American and Far Eastern colonies, doing double duty as ballast on the outbound journeys. The alternating heat and cold the wine was exposed to during the voyages altered the wine. But, surprisingly, it didn't destroy it. In fact, winemakers who tasted the distinctive brew that resulted built special ovens to heat and cool fermented wine to recreate the unique taste. That production method, called the estufa system, is still used.

*W*ine by Any Other Name...

A wine's name is the key to its identity.

What matters most about a particular wine is whether you enjoy drinking it. But if you want to buy it again, or look for similar wines, it helps to be able to put a name with the taste. In fact, what a wine is called can often tell you where, and sometimes how, it was made, and perhaps the grapes it was made from.

There are two basic naming systems, one that eties that generations of trial and error have shown are best suited to that particular area.

For example, wines with the appellation "Bordeaux" are bottled in the Bordeaux region in the southwest of France. Red Bordeaux wines are a blend of some or all of five varieties— cabernet sauvignon, merlot, cabernet franc, malbec, and petit verdot— that are grown in that region. Once you're familiar with the flavors and aromas of a Bordeaux,

identifies a wine by **appellation**, or place name, and another that names wines for the dominant grape—in wine-making terms, the variety— they're made with. Many wines are named using one convention, some are named using both, and a few are named altogether differently.

A PLACE TO CALL HOME

Many European wines are named for the region where they're made, and sometimes for the specific estate within that region, in compliance with a very explicit set of laws. But in many cases the appellation also tells you the variety or varieties of grapes, even though they aren't specifically named. That's because certain European winemaking regions may grow only the grape vari-

you know what to expect from another bottle of Bordeaux even though the grape varieties aren't printed on the label and the proportions may vary.

But no naming system is as simple as this description makes it sound. Within Bordeaux, as in the Chianti region of Italy or the Rioja region of Spain, the climate, soils, and individual wine-making styles of the hundreds of wineries vary somewhat. But, overall, you'll be more aware of the similarities among the wines of these regions than of their differences.

VARIATIONS ON A THEME
A particular type of grape is known as a variety, but a wine made with that variety is known as a varietal.

NAME THAT GRAPE
A different convention is to give a wine a **varietal** name. That's common in the US and in many other winemaking regions of the world, including some parts of Europe.

In the US, regulations allow winemakers to label a wine as a varietal if the wine contains at least 75% of that

grape variety. So when you buy a bottle of zinfandel or sauvignon blanc, you know, at the very least, the basic characteristics you can expect. (The other grapes that are blended into a varietal aren't chosen randomly. Certain grapes are traditionally blended with others to create particular results.)

There are some exceptions to the 75% rule. Oregon requires that a wine identified as a varietal be 90% of that variety (except cabernet sauvignon, where it's 75%). And at the other end of the spectrum, a wine can be labeled concord if at least 51% of the grapes are of the concord variety. That's because concord grapes, which are of the native US species *Vitis labrusca* rather than *Vitis vinifera,* have such intense flavor.

Other non-European countries regulate wine naming practices too, and the rules vary from place to place. For example, Australian rules require a varietal be 85% of that grape variety. Blends are identified as well, so you might find an Australian sémillon-chardonnay.

OTHER WINES, OTHER NAMES
There's no rule without an exception, and that includes the general rule on naming wines.

US wines don't always have varietal names. Sometimes that's simply because there's less than 75% of a single grape variety in the wine. In other cases, winemakers prefer to create wines in a particular, consistent style. That often means varying the proportions of different grapes from year to year, or combining grapes in such a way that a single variety may or may not equal 75%.

For example, a winemaker who wanted to make a Bordeaux-style red wine, with any or all of its five classic components, might not meet the 75% requirement. In that case, the winemaker might decide to give the wine a distinctive name and not worry about the varietal rules. In fact, that's the case with the flagship wines from several well-known wineries.

Some European wines aren't named by their appellations. Among these exceptions are the wines of Alsace, which have varietal names. So does pinot grigio, an Italian white, and a number of wines from the Languedoc region of France.

RED, WHITE, OR PINK
Color names are the easiest way to categorize wine.

This list will help you distinguish color in other languages:

Language	Red	White
German	Rotwein	Weisswein
Italian	Rosso	Bianco
French	Rouge	Blanc
Spanish	Tinto	Blanco

What's in a Name?

A name can tell you a lot, if not everything, about a wine.

A single wine may have many names. For example, a wine made in the US at the hypothetical Deon winery in the mythical region called the Arnold Valley might be named as a red wine, a zinfandel, an Arnold Valley zinfandel, a Deon zinfandel, or a Deon Chalk Vineyard zinfandel.

In most cases, the more specific the name, the more it tells you about what you can expect the wine to be like. There may also be a relationship between the level of detail in the name and the quality of the wine, though it won't necessarily tell you whether you'll enjoy drinking it or not.

NAMING THE PLACE

US wine producers have identified specific wine growing areas—137 of them as of the year 2000—known as American Viticultural Areas (AVA), which are recognized by the Bureau of Alcohol, Tobacco, and Firearms (BATF), the government agency that oversees the wine industry. The goal is to tell you something about the wine by saying where it's from.

An AVA may include several states, a single state, several counties, a single county, or smaller regions within a county. If a producer names a state as the region of origin, all of the grapes must be from that state. When a county is named, 75% of the grapes must come from the county. In smaller AVAs, 85% of the wine in the bottle must have been grown in that AVA. But, there are no rules governing which varieties of grapes can be grown in an AVA.

In Europe, specifically in the countries that are members of the European Union (EU), wine-growing area designations describe not only geographical borders but often the grape varieties, sometimes the time a wine must age

WHAT'S IN A BRAND?

The more specific a wine's name, the more identity it has. A French wine, for example, may carry the name of the specific chateau where the wine was produced and bottled.

In the US, Australia, South America, and other places where names aren't controlled, producers have more latitude. For example, a varietal wine produced by a particular wine grower might be identified by the family name or the winery name, or as the product of a particular vineyard.

Larger producers, who sell many different types of wine from many different places, might brand all of their wines with one name. Individual labels, all carrying that same brand, provide additional information about specific wines. Finally, some wine producers use more than one brand, keeping the one most closely identified with their name or winery for what they consider their best wines. Then they use a second brand for the rest of their production. Many experts consider these secondary brands first-class values.

Many varieties can have the same brand name

before it's released, and, in some cases, even the type of barrel in which the wine must be aged.

IN THE FACE OF CONVENTIONS

According to international trade laws winemakers can use regional names such as Chablis, Burgundy, or Champagne (in France), Chianti or Barolo (in Italy) and Port only for wines that are made within those specific regions by grapes that were grown there, and meet all of the legal requirements for using the name.

While these controls are, for the most part, respected worldwide, that isn't always the case in the US. Blended wines from a number of different and often inferior grapes are sold as Burgundy, Chablis or Chianti, though, in fact, wine in a jug labeled Burgundy has little or nothing in common with even the most modest bottle entitled to be called a Burgundy, except maybe color.

These inaccurate **generic** names are increasingly being replaced by phrases like "white table wine" and "red table wine" on labels that name only the producer and the state of origin.

HELLO my name is
ARNOLD VALLEY ZINFANDEL

HELLO my name is
RED WINE

HELLO my name is
Deon Chalk Vineyard Zinfandel

HELLO my name is
Deon infandel

PROPRIETARY NAMES

Another variation on the naming game is using what's called a **proprietary** name. Some of these wines are varietals. Others are blends, often because the wine maker is interested in creating a wine with a distinctive style. Unlike a family or winery name, a proprietary name is often chosen to evoke a particular reaction or to designate a wine that the winemaker considers top-of-the-line. Most proprietary wines are made in very small quantities, as a producer's flagship wine, or the signature wine of a well-known winemaker. In general, these wines tend to be expensive.

Reading Wine Labels

Labels are a fascinating mix of style and substance.

Although US wine labels are regulated by the Bureau of Alcohol, Tobacco, and Firearms (BATF), a division of the US Department of the Treasury, you might not guess that from looking at the varied assortment of labels on a wine shop's shelves. But all US wine labels have at least three pieces of information on the front label:

Brand name. The brand name may be a single name or a name combined with a visual image.

Name and address of bottler and federal bonded winery number. If the label uses the phrase "produced and bottled by", at least 75% of the wine has to have been fermented and finished in the place that's named. If it says it was vinted, cellared, blended or perfected and bottled by, the wine was fermented in one place and bottled in another.

Alcohol content. If the alcohol content is less than 14%, the label can say it is table wine, give the actual percentage, or both. Producers have a 1.5% margin for error, so a bottle that says it is 11.5% alcohol may have as little as 10% or as much as 13% alcohol. If the alcohol content is over 14%, as it usually is in dessert wines and fortified wines, the actual percentage must be given and it can vary by only 1%.

LABELS DOWN UNDER

Wine labels from Australia are clear and easy to read.

The date is the **vintage**, or the year the grapes were harvested. At least 85% of the grapes must be from that year. (Remember, the growing season in the southern hemisphere spans two years.)

There's always a **brand** or company name, usually accompanied by a distinctive illustration.

When the wine is a **varietal** or a **blend** of grape varieties, those names appear. The fact that sémillon comes first means that there is more sémillon than chardonnay in this blend.

MOUNT JENKINS
1996
SÉMILLON CHARDONNAY
WESTERN AUSTRALIA

Produced by Mount Jenkins Winery Pty. Ltd.
P.O. Box 204, Maggie River, Australia

750 ML PRODUCT OF AUSTRALIA

13.5% vol

Western Australia is one of five major wine-producing states in Australia, the others being New South Wales, South Australia, Victoria, and the island of Tasmania. Some wine is also produced in the Northern Territories and Queensland. One of those names always appears on the label.

In some cases, the label may also name a much smaller, often highly regarded, wine producing region. Examples include the Hunter Valley in New South Wales or the Barossa Valley in South Australia. Those designations provide additional clues about where the grapes were grown and where the wines were made.

Every label also says "Product of Australia" and provides the producer's address, though not necessarily the location of the winery. The percentage of **alcohol** and the size of the bottle are also included.

If a **vintage** is included, 95% of a wine must come from grapes harvested that year. The remaining 5% often comes from wine that winemakers use to top off barrels as they age, to compensate for the evaporation that takes place.

If the wine is a **varietal**, the wine must have at least 75% of the grape variety. If there is a specific sub-category of origin, it will be an American Viticultural Area (AVA), a geographical feature, vineyard or estate name. When it's a vineyard or estate, the grapes that produce the wine must come from that location.

Current BATF labeling regulations allow the potential for confusion between brand name and grape origin. Many of us in the wine industry believe that if a brand name indicates an area of viticultural significance, such as Napa or Sonoma, for example, that the grapes used to produce the wine should come from that area.

—*Tom Shelton*
Joseph Phelps Vineyards

Wine Labels, Continental Style

If you know what to look for, you can find lots of information.

The European place-naming, or appellation, system is also a ranking system. Laws in each country dictate the language that can be used to describe where a bottle of wine was produced. Overall, the general rule is that the more specific the details about the place a wine is from and the smaller that place is, the higher the wine's quality.

French labels that say *Appellation d'Origine Contrôlée* (AC or AOC) are a reliable guide to high-quality wines, and the information they provide is strictly controlled. Other national systems are evolving in the same direction. That's true, for example, of the *Denominazione d'Origine Controllata* (DOC) and *Denominazione di Origine Controllata e Garantita* (DOCG) designation on Italian wines, and *Denominaciones de Origen Calificada* (DOCa) on Spanish wines.

FRENCH LABELS

French wine labels, which all say "Product of France" somewhere on the label, vary enormously from producer to producer and region to region. But there are certain pieces of information you will learn to recognize.

Grand cru classé is an officially classified AOC growth within a particular region, in this case Sauternes. Other classifications you may encounter are premier cru, premier grand cru, cru bourgeois.

Vintage is the year the grapes were grown and harvested. If there's no date, the wine contains wine from different vintages. That's more typical with lower-quality still wines than with AOC wines, and common in Champagne.

The **chateau name**, in this case a hypothetical one, is the name of the producer.

Appellation Sauternes Contrôlée indicates wine that meets a specific set of quality standards established for fine wines made in the specific region. In other regions, such as Burgundy, the most specific locations are often names of villages.

Volume is required. In this case, it's a standard-sized bottle, or 75 cl (which is the same as 750 ml). So is **alcohol content**.

GRAND CRU CLASSÉ

PRODUCT

OF FRANCE

Château Langote

1990

SAUTERNES

APPELLATION SAUTERNES CONTRÔLÉE

Robert Jeune • Viticulteur
à Saint Surtris, France

75 cl

12% vol

The **name and address of bottler** is required on all labels. When the wine is bottled on the grower's property, the label says *mis en bouteille au chateau*. That's generally an indication of quality.

THE PLEASURES OF WINE

A great wine has to come from vines that are more than 25 years old, with grapes of sufficient concentration and complexity. We use grapes from younger vines, with more immediate charm and less opulence, for our second label wines.

—Jean Guillaume Prats
Domaines Prats SA
Chateau Cos d'Estournel

ITALIAN LABELS

Many Italian wine labels, like their French counterparts, may provide information about the quality of the wine as well as the details about where it was made and, in some cases, the name of the grape variety. The rule of thumb is that the more specific the information, the higher the wine's quality.

When the wine is exported, the labels also say "Product of Italy."

Castello di Bossan is the name of the producer, which is often the wine's brand.

Riserva means that the wines were aged long enough to earn this legal designation. It's generally understood as an indication of high quality.

Barolo is the key word on this label. It's the name of a region in the Piedmont region of northern Italy known for its superior wines made from the nebbiolo grape.

Denominazione d'Origine Controllata e Garantita (DOCG) indicates that this wine meets the standards required for the production of the wine in its area of origin.

The **vintage** is the year the grapes were grown. At least 85% of the wine must be from that vintage.

The **producer** or **bottler** is named. In this case, the wine was bottled at the producer's estate.

The **alcoholic content**—in this case 13%—and the **volume** are required on all bottles.

CASTELLO ᴹ DI BOSSAN

Riserva

Barolo

Denominazione d'origine Controllata e Garantita

1994

Imbottigliato all'origine"
de Castello di Bossan"
Prodotto in Italia

ò vol

e 0.750 cl

The DOC and DOCG laws have done a great deal to improve the quality of Italian wines. DOC controls the volume of grape production, and DOCG controls the amount and quality of wine that can be made with the grapes.

—Aldo Conterno, Poderi Aldo Conterno

Red Wine Grapes

Red wine is made from several thousand grape varieties and clones.

A number of the most popular varieties of red-wine grapes—sometimes called black grapes—are cultivated in the US. Some, like zinfandel and cabernet sauvignon, have a long history, while others, like sangiovese and syrah, have only recently been introduced.

Some varieties have been identified with premium wines from the beginning—in fact that is why many of them were planted in the first place. Others that are now made into attractive and pleasing varietals may in the past have been used solely in blends. So it's always smart to try a varietal you may never have heard of. You may be on the cutting edge of a new market.

ALICANTE BOUSCHET

One of the few red-wine grapes that has red juice, alicante bouschet was popular during Prohibition, not only for its rich, deep color but because the hearty grapes could survive shipping to home winemakers. Large producers in the US use the variety in their red-wine blends. A few premium US wineries make a varietal, often blending it with zinfandel. In Europe, it is used as a blending grape to add color.

Alicante Bouschet

Cabernet Sauvignon

CABERNET SAUVIGNON

Widely described as the king of red wine grapes, cabernet sauvignon is probably the most highly regarded variety in the world. Typically, the wines have a complex structure, a rich, deep taste, and lots of tannin. A native of France, it's the most important component in the classic Bordeaux wines. In the US, it's often the flagship wine of premium wineries.

> We all felt a dizzying sense of vertigo that summer day that we planted our first syrah grapevines. It felt as though we were standing on the precipice of something great and forward thinking. Some of our contemporaries scoffed, others guffawed. We stood in silence, wineglasses filled to the brim with a fine Hermitage, and toasted our future.
>
> —*Andrew J. Murray*
> *Andrew Murray Vineyards*

Merlot

MERLOT

The merlot grape produces rich, fruity, deeply-colored wine that is less tannic than cabernet sauvignon, and so more appealing to some drinkers. A native of France, merlot is an important component of the classic Bordeaux blends, and the primary variety in the wines of Pomerol and St. Emilion. In the US, a number of premium wineries produce world-class merlots. It is often blended with cabernet sauvignon to provide more complex and friendly wines.

PETITE SIRAH

The petite sirah grape produces wine that is often described as firm and robust. While petite sirah is grown in more limited quantities in the US than it was 30 years ago, it is both made as a varietal and blended with zinfandel and other grapes to create more rounded wines.

PINOT NOIR

Pinot noir grapes are used to make the rich, velvety red wines of Burgundy. Many premium US wineries also produce pinot noir. There's general

Pinot Noir

agreement, though, that this finicky variety needs more perfect growing conditions to produce outstanding wine than some other varieties and provides greater challenges to the winemaker.

SANGIOVESE

Sangiovese, the primary variety in Chianti—one of the best-known Italian regional wines—is also increasingly popular as a varietal, both from Italian producers and a limited number of US wineries. Flavors and aromas can vary significantly, with some bottles light-bodied and fruity and others full-bodied and more intense.

Sangiovese

SYRAH

The syrah grape, known in Australia and South Africa as shiraz after its Iranian place of origin, is a premium varietal in many winemaking regions of the world, including the US. The wines, which typically have a lot of tannin, are described with the same terms used for cabernet sauvignon and merlot. Hermitage, a wine of the northern Rhone Valley, is made entirely from syrah grapes.

ZINFANDEL

The history of the zinfandel grape is almost as long and varied as the history of US winemaking. Some 100-year old vines are the source of rich, fruity reds that some people consider on a par with the best red wines. Zinfandel grapes are also used to make the extremely popular, if misleadingly named, white zinfandel. But when you see zinfandel as the varietal name, the wine should be red.

White Wine Grapes

Like red wines, white wines are made from many varieties and clones.

Though dozens of white wine grapes are grown in the US, more vineyard space is planted in chardonnay than any other type. That's the direct result of the enormous popularity it enjoys with all types of consumers.

As a change of pace, you might want to experiment with several varieties that aren't as widely known but make extremely pleasing wines. Among them are roussanne, marsanne and viognier.

Chenin Blanc

Chardonnay

rather sweet. That's the case in France as well, in wines like Savennières and Vouvray. In the US, chenin blanc is used in mass-produced blends but is also made as a varietal wine.

COLOMBARD

The high-yielding colombard grape rivals chardonnay in production volume but not flavor, quality, complexity, or longevity. The wines are often pleasing

CHARDONNAY

Chardonnay grapes, which prosper around the globe, produce the exceptional dry white wines that have helped identify the US—California in particular—as a world-class producer of fine wine. Chardonnay, which is made in a variety of styles to appeal to many tastes and pocketbooks, is also a primary component of premium US sparkling wines. In France, Chablis, Pouilly-Fuissé, and other whites of Burgundy are produced from chardonnay grapes.

CHENIN BLANC

An ancient variety, chenin blanc grapes are made into many different wines, from quite dry and crisp to

Colombard

and easy to enjoy, as they tend to be crisp and slightly floral. They're used primarily as blending grapes for generic wines.

Gewürztraminer

GEWÜRZTRAMINER

Best known for their distinctive floral and spicy aroma, gewürztraminer grapes are used to make many styles of wine, from dry and crisp to sweet. Fans consider it a perfect match for a wide variety of food, including intensely flavored or spicy dishes. Some of the most highly regarded gewürztraminer is produced in Alsace, in France.

RIESLING

Riesling grapes are used to make wines that age well, with delicate, distinctive fruity and floral bouquet and flavors. While many people think of rieslings as sweet, they may also be extremely dry and crisp. The best rieslings, from the great wine growing areas of Germany, rival the greatest white wines of the world. Winemakers also make outstanding sweet dessert wines from rieslings.

SAUVIGNON BLANC

These grapes yield wines with distinctive herbal aromas, which are made by many premium wineries in the US, in the Sancerre and Pouilly-Fumé regions of France, and in New Zealand. Lighter and more delicate than chardonnays, they are also frequently less expensive than the chardonnay offered by the same US producer.

SÉMILLON

In recent years, US winemakers, as well as those in France and Australia, have begun to use the sémillon grape to make interesting dry varietals. In the past it was sometimes considered at its best in sweet dessert wines produced from fruit that had been infected with the *Botrytis cinerea* fungus. Sémillion is also frequently blended with sauvignon blanc or, in Australia, with chardonnay.

VIOGNIER

The viognier grape, from the northern Rhone Valley of France, is fairly new to California. The varietal wines produced by a number of premium wineries are attracting lots of interest for their rich textures, floral bouquet, melon flavors, and easy drinkability.

Viognier

The best wines, from the best sites, are unique expressions of those sites. In the new world, with young vineyards that are just developing, sometimes it is better to blend from different vineyards to achieve depth and harmony with a regional style.

—*Jim Clendenen*
Au Bon Climat

A Winemaking Glossary

You'll find some familiar words have different meanings.

CLONE

A clone is a vine of any grape variety that has been developed to replicate a specific characteristic of the vine from which it was propagated. Clones can be created to be disease-resistant, to produce higher or lower yields, to thrive in a particular climate, and for any other characteristic that will contribute to wine production. A clone is often identified by a number or a name, which is known as its clonal designation.

CRUSH

The harvest season is known as the crush. It's a literal description of one phase of winemaking, but it also gives a sense of the excitement everyone feels at harvest time.

CUVÉE

A cuvée is a blend, which can include as few as two or three or as many as 30 to 40 different lots of wine. The term is used most often to describe the blend for a sparkling wine, though it may be used for other wines. A cuvée may include fruit from different varietals, vintages, or vineyards.

MOUSSE

The steady stream of bubbles, or effervescence, in a sparkling wine is known as its mousse. There's general agreement that the smaller the bubbles and the more persistent the stream, the more pleasing the wine. You'll discover though, that each style of sparkling wine has a distinctive mousse.

We feel a great obligation to act as responsible stewards of the Eisele Vineyard.™ This is not just a vineyard, but an important part of Napa Valley's history. Not to do everything within our power to nurture this special place on earth would be unthinkable...and the more we invest of ourselves physically and spiritually, the more the Eisele Vineyard seems to give back to us.

—*Bart and Daphne Araujo*
Araujo Estate Wines

NÉGOCIANT

Someone who buys wine after fermentation and stores it until it is bottled and sold to wholesale or retail customers is called a négociant. The négociant oversees the aging, racking, blending, and bottling of the wine, and may control the winemaking from crush as well.

> Making wine is a combination of science and magic. It's agricultural business and art form. For example, as harvest approaches, we weigh the climatic conditions. We sample sugar levels by picking three berries from every third vine and crushing them by hand in a food-mill. But we make the final decisions about when to pick the grapes based on instinct.
>
> *—Anne Hargrave*
> *Castello di Borghese/*
> *Hargrave Vineyard*

POMACE

The seeds, skins, and stems left behind after grapes have been pressed is described as pomace. In Italy it's distilled into a brandy called grappa. More often, it's spread around in the vineyards as a natural fertilizer, to add nutrients to the soil.

RESERVE

In some countries, a wine must meet strict aging requirements to qualify to be labelled reserve. That's true in both Italy and Spain, for example. In other countries, including the US, the term is used more flexibly. While some producers put the term reserve on a label to indicate wines they consider superior, others use it strictly as a marketing device, often for lesser quality wines.

RESIDUAL SUGAR

Residual sugar is natural grape sugar that's not fermented to alcohol. It's most characteristic in dessert wines, which are made from grapes whose high sugar levels inhibit a complete conversion, or fermentation. What keeps these wines from being too sweet is that they typically have high natural acid levels to balance the sugar. In contrast, you may find mass-produced wines that are deliberately made with residual sugar too sweet for your taste.

OAKY

Wine that has been fermented or aged in oak barrels takes on distinctive flavors and aromas, some from the oak itself and some that result from the wood's being charred, or toasted. But when a wine is described as oaked, or, more commonly, over-oaked, the implication is that the flavors of the oak overpower the flavors of the wine. Sometimes, oak chips or shavings are added to lesser wines after fermentation and before filtration, to add flavors and aromas artificially without the expense of oak barrels and the time required to extract the nuances that barrels add naturally. While it's legal in some places, including the US, the practice is frowned on as being artificial.

The Pleasures of Wine

Enjoying wine isn't a test, and there's no passing score.

Did you ever wonder why people often seem uneasy when the subject of wine comes up?

How many times have you heard a friend say that she doesn't know anything about wine? And how often have you said the same thing yourself, especially when it's your job to order wine in a restaurant, or choose a bottle to take to dinner?

The fact is, many people are convinced that everybody else knows a lot more than they do about how to choose a "good" wine, or how to recognize a "good" wine when they taste one.

VARIETY...THE SPICE OF LIFE... AND CONFUSION

Part of the reason choosing wine can be a little intimidating is sheer variety, since there are so many wines, made by so many winemakers in so many different countries.

Then consider that two wines made with the same grape variety, but by different winemakers, won't taste exactly alike. And two bottles made by the same winemaker in different years won't taste exactly alike either.

In contrast, mass-produced wines—non-vintage wines made in large volume—are deliberately made to taste the same from bottle to bottle, and from year to year. With that exception, you can't choose wine the way you might choose a particular soft drink, a kind of beer, or a brand of orange juice.

Age also affects wine. Some wines taste best when they're young. Others are aged for years, or even decades, before they reach their peak.

Finally, there's cost. There are many delicious wines in the $8 to $12 range, although others do cost more. A few may even be hundreds of dollars.

THE TASTE OF WINE

The way wine tastes depends on three essential factors:
- Which grapes were used to make it
- Where the grapes grew
- Who made the wine

Whether you like the wine depends on your reaction to that taste.

The best wine in the world is the one you like the most.

—*Brad Kane*
Garnet Wines & Liquors

Wine is about flavor and pleasure, not rules and dogma.

—*Dan Philips*
The Grateful Palate

A Taste Test

Just a sip of wine can be a totally sensuous experience.

When you drink wine, you engage at least four of your senses—sight, smell, feel, and of course, taste. And if you listen for the distinctive pop of the cork as it slides out of the bottle, the splash of liquid being poured into your glass, or the faint effervescence of sparkling wine, then sound is the fifth sense that contributes to your pleasure.

The impression a wine makes as you raise your glass, sniff the wine, and take a first sip tends to be a lasting one, even though the aroma and flavors change as you drink. In fact, you probably form a positive impression ("This is delicious") or a negative one ("I don't like this") in the first few moments the wine is in your mouth.

Understanding the factors that influence your sensory reactions may increase your appreciation even more, since it can help you decide not only if you enjoy what you've tasted, but the reasons you feel the way you do.

TASTING, ONE STEP AT A TIME

Tasting wine fully is both simple and fun. Each step along the way— looking, swirling, smelling, sipping, and swallowing—isolates and focuses on one distinctive element, from how the wine looks when you pour it from the bottle, to how it tastes at the finish, which is the lingering impression you're left with after you've swallowed the wine. You actually use a similar process in tasting food, especially when it's beautifully presented, and has a rich aroma and distinctive flavors.

You'll also quickly discover that each step in the wine-tasting process flows naturally into the next. The more often you taste wine this way, the more aware you'll become of the relationship between how a wine looks and the way it smells, the link between the way it tastes initially on your tongue and later at the back of your mouth.

Hear the wine

See the wine

Smell the wine

Taste the wine

GETTING BETTER ALL THE TIME

There are lots of good reasons to become comfortable with the tasting process. In the first place, there's no better way to demystify what sometimes can seem like an elaborate ritual. And while there's a certain amount you can learn from reading about what to look for in a wine, you really learn to recognize a wine's unique qualities only by tasting it.

For example, you can begin to understand, based on look, smell, feel, and taste, what distinguishes one wine from another. And you gradually build your wine memory. That means you can identify a wine without knowing its name because you recognize its distinctive characteristics—the way you can recognize a songwriter's music or a painter's style.

FINDING FAULTS

The tasting process can also identify a wine that's faulty. If a wine doesn't look right—a young white is more brownish than pale wheat-colored—or it doesn't smell right—more like nail polish remover than fruit—that's often an indication there's a problem and you may not enjoy drinking it.

Just as recognizing those things you like, and being able to explain what they are, can help you find another wine that's likely to please you, knowing what doesn't please you can be equally useful in making wine choices.

And, on those (rare) occasions when a bottle is spoiled, being able to recognize and explain what's unpleasing can give you the confidence you need to reject a bottle in a restaurant, or return it to a wine merchant.

THE TIMING OF TASTING

It goes without saying that you should taste a wine before you drink it if you're the one who has ordered the wine in a restaurant or opened a bottle for family or guests. After the wine passes that initial test, and you pour, others may want to taste the wine as well. It can be a perfect opportunity to introduce the process to people who've only recently started to learn and talk about wine.

Remember, though, that tasting is something you do with the first sips of a wine. It's not the same as lingering over a bottle, sometimes enjoying the way the flavors and the bouquet change—though tasting may often be the first stage of that experience.

A PRIVATE RITUAL

Don't be put off by the fact that some people make tasting a very formal ritual—full of intent gazes, deep meditation, and serious pronouncements—perhaps as a dribble of wine slips from the corner of their mouths. Instead, think of tasting as a way to savor a treat or make a pleasure last. And if you're pleased by what you discover about a wine's taste, you can have the immediate satisfaction of another sip.

WHY THE FUSS?

At some level, you're testing the wine you're tasting each time you open a new bottle, whether or not you've ever tasted that wine before. You do the same thing each time you take the first bite of a new or favorite dish. If it's a wine you know, and perhaps recommended to friends, does it live up to what you remember? Or, if it's been recommended to you, does it meet your expectations?

Since no two people's tastes are exactly alike, and since you have so much choice, there's no reason to buy a second bottle of a wine that doesn't satisfy you the first time. But there's also no way to know what you like without trying new wines and discovering new tastes.

> The thing to remember about your perception of taste and smell is that they are essentially one because you always do some of both simultaneously. It's like the old philosophical quandary of mind and body. You could argue that they are distinct but the intimate interconnectedness is undeniable.
>
> What we "taste" is often a tactile or "feel" sensation. When, for instance, you proclaim a wine to be tannic or full-bodied, you are really feeling those characteristics with your mouth, not really tasting. You see what kind of trouble you can get into by asking an out of practice philosopher to "demystify" things.
>
> —*Tony Soter, Etude Wines*

$\mathcal{L}$ook Before You Sip

Part of the pleasure of tasting wine is anticipating what's coming.

Believe it or not, more than half the wine tasting process is over before you take your first sip. And by the time you're done—a matter of seconds—you've probably discovered enough about a wine to be fairly certain whether you'll enjoy it or not. You may also be able to anticipate at least some of the taste sensations it will provide.

Until you've done it a few times, the wine-tasting process may seem more trouble than it's worth. Or it may seem like a lot of hokum. But you'll be amazed at how quickly it can become second nature, and how much it can add to the pleasure of drinking wine.

HERE'S LOOKING AT WINE

You don't look at wine to determine if you're drinking a white wine, a rosé, or a red, but to make some preliminary observations about the taste you anticipate, or the wine's age and even quality.

CLARIFYING CLARITY

With white wine, even a quick look will tell you the wine's **clarity**, which may be an important indicator of the wine's quality. What clarity means, however, isn't always clear.

In the first place, the differences in the descriptive phrases "clear", "translucent", and "slightly cloudy" can be quite subjective.

Second, while cloudiness can be a defect—the result of improper storage or bacterial growth—it can also be the natural result of producing wine. Some winemakers choose not to fine or filter wine before they bottle it, describing their method as a more natural process that retains more distinctive wine fla-

vors. As a result, unfiltered wine is different in style though not necessarily in quality. And, it's likely to be somewhat cloudy.

In fact, some experts argue that modern production methods are reliable enough to produce perfectly clear wine all the time, if that's what a winemaker intends. So clarity as an indicator of wine quality means much less now than it may have in the past.

THE COLOR OF TASTE

The color of wine can often tell you something about how the wine will taste, especially how rich or full-bodied it may be.

The visual impact of two white wines of similar age, one that's a deep golden color and another that resembles pale wheat, may suggest that the first will be more full-bodied than the second, or that the second may be lighter and crisper than the first.

Different colors can be the result of different grape varieties, different wine making practices, or the wine's age—or some combination of these. For example, a chardonnay usually is a deeper color than a sauvignon blanc or a riesling.

You can see similar color differences in red wine as well, which can run the gamut from bright, light red to an almost opaque black pearl. The color of a Beaujolais, for instance, is usually lighter and less concentrated

COLOR CAN DETERMINE TASTE

than that of a cabernet sauvignon. In other words, a darker, deeper color usually indicates a more full-bodied wine than one that is lighter and more translucent.

THE COLOR OF AGE
Color can also indicate a wine's age. Most white wines deepen in color as they get older, from almost clear or pale gold to a deeper golden. So a ten-year-old chardonnay will usually be a deeper color than the current vintage from the same producer, though it may be equally (or even more) delicious. The natural maturing process changes the smell and taste as well, often adding complexity and depth to the wine.

If a wine isn't the color you expect, your first reaction may be that there's something wrong with the wine. For example, what if a young white wine is a deep golden color? The wine may turn out to be delicious, though it may also be

spoiled. Only smelling and tasting it will tell. On the other hand, a white wine that's more brown than golden usually indicates that there is a problem. In that case, the wine may not be drinkable, whatever its age.

Color can alert you to potential problems with red wines, too. A young red wine that looks brownish may not taste good. On the other hand, some delicious older reds may pick up brick, brown, and garnet tones as part of the aging process. Rather than being a warning sign, this change in color may indicate that considerable time has passed since the wine was bottled and additional pleasing flavors have developed.

COLOR DEEPENS WITH AGE

The color of wine is like its face. It can, for the most part, tell us its age as well as give us a glimpse of its character. Look at a glass of wine and drink it with your eyes first.

—*Greg Lill*
DeLille Cellars

Giving Wine Some Air

Wine comes alive when it breathes, and you can help the process along.

Swirling is the second step in the tasting process. Like looking, it too occurs before you lift your glass.

You swirl by holding the bottom of the stem between your thumb and fingers, resting your hand near or on the foot of the glass, and gently rotating the glass on the table top to expose the maximum surface area of the wine to air. Swirling is important because it allows the wine to breathe, and breathing helps to bring out the nuances of smell and taste.

Now you know, too, why using a small glass or filling a wine glass to the brim are bad ideas. You can't swirl the wine (without spilling it), so you don't have a chance to help the wine breathe.

IS THERE A RIGHT WAY TO SWIRL?

Should you move the wine glass clockwise or counterclockwise when you swirl your wine? The answer depends on personal (and perhaps cultural) preferences, not the physics of motion. Choosing either direction, you achieve the result you're after. So try it both

AND IF YOU CAN'T SWIRL

If you order wine by the glass rather than by the bottle, you've probably had the experience of being served one that's full to the brim. Obviously, there's no way to swirl the wine or take a sniff without risking disaster. Short of asking if there's a larger glass you could use, there's probably not much you can do to correct the situation.

This type of overpouring is often an attempt—however mistaken—of trying to make customers happy by seeming to give them their money's worth. In fact, the practice may have grown out of having to explain to irate patrons why the restaurant had the nerve to serve a half-full glass of wine.

CLEANLINESS IS NEXT TO . . .

If your wine bubbles and foams when you swirl it, or if it doesn't create legs, the problem may be that you didn't rinse the glass carefully enough the last time you washed it.

DEMYSTIFYING WINE

LOOKING FOR BODY

As you swirl the wine in your glass, the liquid moves up and around the bowl and slides down the inside walls. The beautiful visual patterns that result are known as the wine's **legs**. These patterns develop, it's generally believed, because the alcohol and glycerine in the wine create surface tension along the glass.

In general, legs are a good indication of what to expect in the wine's body, or texture. The thicker or more viscous the legs, and the more slowly they move down the side of the glass, the higher the sugar or alcohol levels in the wine. That means the wine is likely to be full-bodied. Dessert wines, for example, which have higher sugar levels than table wines, may also leave distinctive, viscous, patterns on the sides of the glass.

In contrast, the less obvious and less viscous the legs, the more likely the wine is to be light-bodied.

PROTECT THOSE BUBBLES

While you can break many rules in enjoying wine, some experts believe that you should never swirl a sparkling wine. You risk dissipating the bubbles. And without bubbles, the smell and flavors may remain, but the sparkle is gone.

Others argue that *méthode champenoise* wines can benefit by swirling. It's a difference of opinion that you'll have to resolve for yourself.

ways, and see which feels more natural to you.

Chances are if you're right-handed, moving the glass counterclockwise will be more comfortable.

If you're left-handed, a clockwise motion might work better. In both cases, the motion is inward, toward you, rather than away.

As you learn more about wine—how it looks, how it smells, how it tastes—some of the mystery that surrounds it disappears, but none of the romance.

Take your time with wine. Pour it into a wonderful, big glass. Look at it. Enjoy the beauty of the wine: the color, the brilliance, the rim. Smell it, hold the glass by its stem.

Learn the words people use when they talk about wine, because if there's one thing we like to do more than drink wine, it's to talk about it.

—*Yvonne Rich*
Wine educator

The Nose Knows

Call it sniffing, or inhaling if you prefer, but take the time to smell the wine.

In many ways, smelling is the most important step in the wine tasting process. In fact, in tasting wine, as in tasting any other food or beverage, the way something smells is a major factor in determining what you taste.

To smell a wine, lift the glass you have swirled, put your nose into the bowl of the glass and take a short, deep sniff. If you like, repeat the process one or more times—swirling, sticking your nose in the glass, and inhaling sharply. By the time you take your first sip, your enjoyment of the wine has already begun.

TRUSTING WHAT YOU SMELL

The more experience you have tasting wine, the more you'll realize how important smell can be both in detecting a wine that won't please you and identifying one that will.

Basically, if the smell is unpleasing, the taste probably will be as well. And conversely, if the smell is pleasing, the same should be true of the taste.

Actually, this nearly infallible relationship works on two levels. First, a really bad smell will help you identify a spoiled bottle. Odors of burnt matches, wet cardboard, and nail polish remover, among other unpleasant smells, are signs of a wine gone bad. You can probably forego the trouble of actually tasting a wine that smells like that. The one reason to take a sip would be to see if the unpleasant odor blows off after time in the glass, providing an unexpected pleasure. That can happen in certain cases, generally in a short period of time. The longer the unpleasant smell lingers, the less likely it will ever disappear.

Second, since the point of smelling isn't usually to ferret out a bad bottle, but to distinguish an acceptable wine from a truly exceptional one, you're more apt to learn from the way a wine smells how likely you are to be pleased with it.

AROMA, THEN BOUQUET

Are you confused by the difference between a wine's **aroma** and its **bouquet**? You're not alone, since many people use the words interchangeably. One easy way to remember the difference is that A comes before B. Aromas are individual, primary smells of the grapes and juice before fermentation occurs. Aromas evolve into the complex smells that are described as bouquet. Even after the wine is bottled, its bouquet and its flavors continue to develop and change.

The bouquet is not a separate or distinct aroma but rather the result of

NAME TAGS FOR SMELLS

Most of the pleasing bouquets you're likely to detect in wine are a combination of various smells. The list below is just a sampling of the impressions you may have when you smell a wine. The same words, and others, are often used to describe flavors as well.

Earthy
mushrooms, dried leaves, forests, truffles

Fruity cherries, raspberries, blackberries, plums, apples, pears

Animal
gamey, wet fur, bacon fat

aromas layered together and combined into a new, often richer smell. Put another way, aromas are the component parts of bouquet before they come together, and a bouquet is more than the sum of those parts.

THE TASTE CONNECTION

Smelling is important to appreciating wine, and like the other steps in the process, it takes only a second or two.

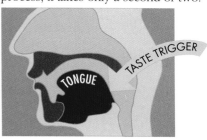

The part of your brain that houses your ability to taste, the olfactory center, gets most of its input from sensors located in your nose and the back of your throat, rather than from your mouth. As the food or drink you are about to put into your mouth passes your nose, those sensors send signals to the brain that trigger your expectations of what you are about to taste.

> The tasting experience is one that combines our olfactory (smelling) experience with our gustatory (tasting) experience. By the time a sip of wine hits our tongue, our brain has already conveyed to our mouth and reflexly back to our brain what we are about to taste. The taste buds, which are located throughout our tongue in different concentrations in different locations, confirm what we are tasting. The biggest and most sensitive of those taste buds (the papillae) are located at the back of the tongue.
>
> —*Maurice T. Zagha, MD*

Spicy cinnamon, mint, eucalyptus, allspice, black pepper, cloves

Herbal freshly cut grass, bell pepper, celery, artichoke

Sweet vanilla (often the result of oak aging), chocolate, butterscotch, creme caramel

Floral violets, rose petals, citrus blossoms, gardenia

These distinctive sensations of smell aren't figments of your imagination. While there aren't actually any raspberries in the wine, the smell of raspberry is produced by the complex chemical components that exist in the wine, which share characteristics with the complex chemical components in raspberries.

Remember, though, that the sense of smell often triggers very personal reactions. You may be aware of something quite different from the person across the table, even though you are tasting the same wine. One reason is that people may have very different impressions and memories of what something smells like. Another is that people express what they are sensing with different words, so that what seems like pears to one person might seem like nectarines to another.

Treating Your Tastebuds

One sip of wine can spark an entire parade of distinctive tastes.

SWEET

There's no special technique for taking a sip. Just do what you always do. In fact, a normal sip is ideal. You don't want too much in your mouth, because you want to be able to move the wine around. And you don't want too little, because the heat of your mouth can volatize the alcohol and overshadow the taste of the wine.

After you sip, wash the wine around in your mouth, so that it covers the entire surface. You can slosh it if that appeals to you, or you can be a little more subtle, moving the wine gently over your tongue, the insides of your cheeks, and across the roof of your mouth. As the wine reaches the back of your mouth, your smell receptors, sometimes called aroma sensors, bring out the taste even more fully.

Moving the wine around aerates and gently warms it, which helps to bring out its flavors. By analogy, think about the moment at which an especially delicious ice cream tastes best. Generally, it's after you've held it in your mouth just long enough to warm it slightly and release its full flavor. You're seeking the same perfect moment when you taste wine.

TASTEBUDS

You can taste certain differences in food and wine because your tastebuds perform highly specialized jobs in distinguishing sweetness, acidity, saltiness, and bitterness. Your tastebuds help explain why, when you take a sip of wine, you experience the taste sensations you do in a particular sequence.

Your first taste impression tells you whether the wine is sweet or not, since the tastebuds for sweetness are located on the tip of your tongue. Wines with a high sugar content taste sweet, while the absence of sugar creates a taste that wine drinkers describe as dry. A wine that's somewhere in between, not really sweet but not really dry, is described as medium dry.

As the wine—white wine in particular—touches the sides of your tongue, you may become aware of an acidic, or sour, taste since that's where the tastebuds that react to acid are located. You'll hear the term **crisp**, or sometimes **tart**, used to describe a wine that's pleasingly acidic.

Pleasing acidity isn't as strange a concept as it may seem. A wine's acidity often produces its distinctive taste. And acidity is one of the factors that helps determine how the wine will age and how well its flavors will go with certain foods.

THE TASTE OF TANNIN

Like acids, **tannin** exists naturally in grapes, and affects the taste of wine. Since tannin is concentrated in the grape skins and seeds, which are present when red wine (but not white wine) is fermented, tannin is more

apparent in reds. Tannin is also found in the oak of oak barrels, and some tannin is extracted during barrel aging, increasing the total tannin in any red (or white) wine aged in oak.

Both tannin and acid can make your mouth feel dry. (Don't confuse this meaning of dry with the use of dry to describe a wine that is not sweet.) The sense of dryness caused by tannin—sometimes described as a puckery feeling—tends to linger in your mouth after you swallow, while the dryness of acid is offset by the saliva that your mouth produces.

BREATHE IN TO BRING OUT FLAVOR

After you've sipped the wine, inhale gently, drawing air into your mouth. (You might want to practice this step once or twice in private and you can try it with water if you don't want to practice with wine.)

Complexity in wine is usually an acquired taste. But in my experience, there are always a few wines that straddle the line, which everyone can appreciate.

—*Steve Plotnicki*
Astor Place Recordings

Adding air as you're moving the wine around in your mouth serves the same function as swirling the wine in your glass before you smell it. It introduces air into the wine—the technical term is aeration. That added air helps to release the flavors and intensify the impression that the wine makes in your mouth.

Holding the wine in your mouth for a moment can also warm it and enhance the initial discovery process.

Every Sip Has Its Own Finish

Even swallowing the wine can add more flavor, and prolong the taste.

The final step of the tasting process is swallowing. There aren't any tastebuds in your throat, so you won't experience any new taste sensations. But there are smell sensors at the back of your mouth that reinforce your impression of the wine's bouquet. And your taste buds are still stimulated by the sweet, sour, or bitter flavors of the wine.

As you swallow, you pay attention to how long those flavors of the wine linger in your mouth and nose. What you're considering is known as the wine's **finish**. Simple wines tend to finish simply and fade quickly, while the bouquet and tastes of more complex wines last for several seconds or longer.

A long finish may confirm your impression that the wine was one you found pleasing and reaffirm the reasons you thought so. Or it may remind you of something you didn't especially like—

FRUITY ISN'T SWEET

There's an important distinction between a wine that's sweet—which you recognize when you taste it—and a wine that's fruity—which you recognize when you smell and taste it. The sense of sweetness in a fruity wine comes from your perception of flavors in that wine that you associate with fruit or fruit juice.

that the wine seemed sour or bitter, for example—and suggest that you should taste again to confirm your feelings.

IS SWEET BAD?

One of the first things you may have learned about wine is that good wines are dry. So does that mean sweet wines are bad? Nothing could be less true. Choosing a sweet wine instead of a dry one is a matter of taste, timing, and the food you're eating with the wine.

SOME SWEET WINES

Many people enjoy a moderately sweet wine with certain types of meals or at certain times of the day. A rosé wine that's more sweet than dry can be perfect for a leisurely summer lunch. Similarly, white wines from Germany, Austria, and some other areas are classified as sweet because they have residual sugar. But they go well with food because they also have higher levels of acid, which balance the sweetness and leave you with the perception of fruitiness. The wines that you drink at the end of a meal, usually described as dessert wines, are sweet because of their residual sugar as well.

Fortified wines, such as sherries, which are often served as an aperitif before a meal, or ports, which are often served at the end of the meal,

> 🍷🍷 Ushered in by a wine's texture, the finish is your last and most lasting impression. 🍷🍷
>
> —*Joseph L. Sullivan*
> *The Insiders' Wine Line*

WHAT NOW?

Once you've tasted the wine and formed your initial impression, you may not think about the tasting process again until you open another bottle. But since a wine's flavors can evolve after the bottle has been opened, poured, or decanted, and as its temperature changes, you may decide to repeat the tasting process before all the wine is drunk.

The second tasting may confirm what you thought at first, or it may change your impression for the better—or sometimes the worse. And retasting the wine can give you a chance to evaluate how well the wine seems to suit the food you're eating. If you like the combination, you can match them again. And if you're not convinced they work well together, you can do something different the next time.

TASTING LIKE THE PROS

When wine critics and professional tasters evaluate wine, they follow this process, too. But if they are tasting a number of wines at the same time—in a long sitting that could include anywhere from 20 to 100 wines or more—they often omit the final step, and spit the wine out before swallowing. While its smell and flavor may seem intoxicating, wine can't go to your head if you don't drink it. And since there are no taste buds in your throat, skipping the final step doesn't change a wine's flavor profile for the tasters, and lets them keep their senses of taste and evaluation sharp for the wines to come.

may also be sweet. Fortified means that the grape alcohol produced by distillation is deliberately added to a wine to create a distinctive flavor and raise the alcohol content. If it's added early, the alcohol stops the fermentation process, leaving residual sugar in the wine, and creating the sweetness.

Undoubtedly, there are some very simple sweet wines that you—and other wine drinkers—may not like. They're not very good with food and can be cloying and viscous, leaving your mouth feeling sticky. Or you may find that you liked them once and you don't like them anymore, the way you outgrew marshmallows or crackerjacks.

Balance

Balance means more than walking a tightrope between mixtures of different ingredients.

If there's one characteristic you can single out as essential to the impression a wine makes on you, it's **balance**—or lack of balance. A wine has balance when its flavors, texture, and bouquet complement each other. That means

- Each of the components is recognizable—and pleasing—on its own
- No single component overpowers the others

Balance is not only essential in making a wine enjoyable to drink while it's young. It's also key to the wine's ability to improve with age and grow in complexity. While balance can be somewhat difficult to define, it's easy to detect and enjoy.

ANOTHER VIEW

One way to understand balance is to think about food.

Salad dressings, for example, are balanced when they taste good on your finger and when they're combined with lettuce or other greens. But when one flavor dominates—when all you taste in a vinaigrette is the vinegar, for example—it draws attention to itself, and away from the food. You may have had a similar experience with a lemon pie that's too sour, a chili that's too spicy, or a ham that's too salty.

With wine, as with food, the balance, or lack of it, is the result of the quality of the ingredients and the way it was made. The more familiar you become with the things that are pleasing,

the more comfortable you will be in distinguishing a well-balanced wine.

Remember, though, that a dish that's too intense for you may taste delicious to someone else. The same is true with wine. A person whose taste is different may feel there's a happier marriage of flavors, texture, and bouquet than you do. And, as many people's taste in food changes as they get older or eat a more varied diet, so does their taste in wine.

WHERE BALANCE STARTS

Getting the balance right depends on several factors.

Acid—malic, lactic, and tartaric—is a vital component of a balanced wine. It adds to the impression of freshness and crispness. If the acid levels are too low, the wine will taste more like a soft, flabby, fruit juice. At the same time, if there aren't enough fruit flavors, the wine will be sour and unpleasant.

At the opposite end of the spectrum, sweet wines with lots of residual sugar (sugar that has not fermented to alcohol) can taste almost syrupy unless there's enough natural acidity present to balance the sweetness. If there is, the wine can be extremely pleasing.

LOSING YOUR BALANCE

It will come as no surprise that alcohol contributes to the character of a wine. But it, too, has to be in balance. If the alcohol level is too high, taking a sip may produce a sense of heat, especially after you swallow.

13.5% ALCOHOL

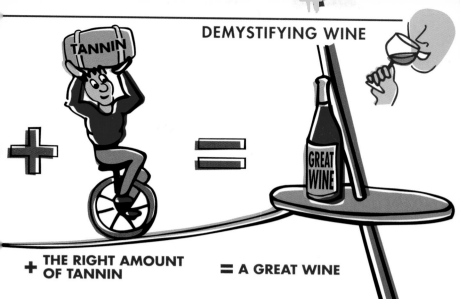

+ THE RIGHT AMOUNT OF TANNIN

= A GREAT WINE

Tannin is another essential factor in creating a balanced wine with the potential to mature into an even better one.

Because tannin is so essential to the aging process, there has sometimes been a tendency to make red wines with high tannin levels in anticipation that they will evolve into delicious bottles later on. However, the fruit dries out in many of these wines long before the tannins mature and soften. Today, balance from the start is far more appreciated, and super-tannic wines are the exception rather than the rule.

To achieve that balance, winemakers allow the grapes to ripen longer—one of the reasons red-wine grapes are usually picked later in the harvest. They may also let the juice remain in contact with the skins for an extended period, so that some of the bitter tannin molecules precipitate out, leaving only the more desireable ones in the liquid. The ripe, soft tannins eventually evolve as the wine ages, which unripe tannins can't, and add even greater complexity.

THE ANATOMY OF WINE
If you find it easier to think of balance in physical terms, think about the way each element in wine can be likened to a living, growing thing. Acid is the backbone, providing the structure that holds everything together. Tannin is the muscle, providing strength and endurance. Fruit is the flesh, or texture.

KEEPING THINGS IN BALANCE
Wines that are well made are balanced and pleasing to drink when they're young and should evolve into similarly balanced and pleasing wines when they mature. You'll be able to identify some of these characteristics:

BALANCE

SWEET

ACID

In contrast, an unbalanced young wine may be drinkable but never totally enjoyable. Nor, as it ages, will it be able to create the balance it lacked to begin with. Telltale signs include:

FRUIT THAT'S HIDDEN OR BURIED BY

TANNINS

Sweetness

that's cloying

Fruit that's overpowered by OAKINESS

Acid that's SOUR or unpleasantly - sharp -

Wine Has Feelings, Too

Describing wine can be a delicate or weighty matter.

Some wines feel soft and smooth in your mouth. Others feel rough or coarse. Some feel thin—as if they had no substance—and others seem almost creamy. Still others feel oily or, at the opposite extreme, almost astringent.

You're not imagining these textures. The grapes a wine is made from and the way the wine is made, as well as its age and how it has been stored, all affect the tactile impression the wine makes in your mouth.

NAMING NAMES

When wine drinkers want to describe the way a wine feels—as opposed to how it smells or tastes—they often compare the feel to a familiar texture. For example, if you taste a wine whose texture is pleasingly soft and smooth, you might use words like velvety or silky. Similarly, you might call an appealing young white wine steely or crisp, and a satisfyingly rich red wine meaty or chewy.

In contrast, if you're disappointed in the wine's texture, you might use words like rough, sharp, or coarse to explain why you don't like it.

While the terms aren't scientific, and tend to be subjective, others sharing the same wine will understand what you're saying, even if they do not have exactly the same impression or choose different words to describe their own reactions to the wine.

Another way you may hear texture described is that some wines are light-bodied while others are medium-bodied, and still others are full-bodied.

You might find it helpful to think about the way other liquids, such as fruit juices, feel in your mouth. But be careful in making these comparisons to concentrate on the feel of the juice, not the flavor.

SIX OF ONE

When one wine seems heavy and another seems light, it's a difference of impression, not a literal difference in weight. Six ounces of one wine weighs the same as six ounces of another, and takes up the same amount of space in your glass.

TIME CHANGES THINGS

Wine is alive and continues to change. It ages in the barrel or tank before it is bottled and in the bottle before you open it. And it can even change, or open up, sitting in your glass. So the way a wine feels at one time may be quite different from the way it feels earlier or later in its life.

Red wines that are extremely high in tannin may feel rough—almost **sandy** or gritty—if you drink them when they are young. But if you drink the same wines when they're more mature, you may find them soft and **velvety**.

Similarly, wine aerates, or breathes, in your glass. A wine that seems sharp or hard when you take a first sip may seem silky after a few minutes in your glass.

So while first impressions are important, changes that happen are mostly for the better.

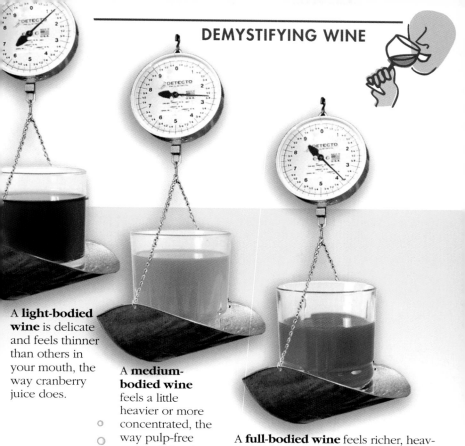

A **light-bodied wine** is delicate and feels thinner than others in your mouth, the way cranberry juice does.

A **medium-bodied wine** feels a little heavier or more concentrated, the way pulp-free orange juice does.

A **full-bodied wine** feels richer, heavier, and more concentrated, the way thick tomato juice or a fruit nectar does.

A TOUCH OF THE BUBBLY

Intentional effervescence, the feel of tiny bubbles bursting in your mouth when you drink a glass of sparkling wine, is for many people one of the world's great pleasures.

Occasionally, though, you may feel a very slight effervescence, or spritz, on your tongue when you're not expecting it—even if you don't see any bubbles in your glass. That's the result of a continued, and usually unwanted, fermentation in the bottle of a still wine.

In most cases this hidden effervescence (called *pétillance*) is a fault, caused either by the way the wine was made and/or the way it was bottled. It's not necessarily harmful but it can be unpleasant. If it is, you may want to return the wine if you've ordered it in a restaurant or take it back to your wine merchant.

WEIGHING IN ON MENUS

Just as your perception of smells and flavors may be different from other people's, so may your impression of weight. So if you're looking at a wine list that's organized by weight, remember that the groupings are only a guide and that the distinctions are subjective. Don't be surprised to discover that a wine listed on one wine list as light-bodied may appear on another as medium-bodied.

HEADY SENSATIONS

In general, alcohol content is a major factor in determining the way wine feels in your mouth. The higher the percentage of alcohol, the richer and more full-bodied the wine seems. But this rule of thumb has some important exceptions.

Wine with higher sugar levels, such as a dessert wine, may feel rich and soft in your mouth because it coats the surfaces. But it doesn't necessarily have a high alcohol level.

Dry wines with high acid levels, such as some sauvignon blancs and other crisp whites, tend to seem lighter in your mouth, especially when they are cold, even though they may have a higher than average alcohol level.

Every Wine Rates

Wines are rated for many reasons, including helping you make a selection you'll enjoy.

You might be intrigued by wine ratings or you might hate them. You might even be conflicted about how you feel, especially if a wine's grades are better than yours ever were. But you'll know how seriously to take wine ratings—or whether you'll be just as happy ignoring them—if you have a sense of what rating and ranking are all about.

A PREMIER RANKING
One of the most famous and influential wine rankings in history occurred in 1855, when the wine brokers of Bordeaux, France, were asked to classify the wines of the region for that year's Paris Exposition. The merchants focused on 61 outstanding wines, dividing them into five growths—or *crus*—based on two fairly objective criteria: The prices they commanded, and the long-term reputation of the chateaux that produced them.

With one exception, when Chateau Mouton Rothschild was elevated to a first growth in 1973, that classification is still intact. So is the distinction of being one of the chosen, despite the fact there are now many outstanding, but unclassified, wines produced, not only in the Bordeaux region but elsewhere in France.

One undeniable impact of the 1855 classification, despite its narrow scope, has been the conviction in many quarters that's its not only possible to identify the best wines, but appropriate to do so.

DEFINING THE RULES
The purpose of rating is to determine whether some wines are superior to others. For a rating system to work, you need to define what you mean by superior and establish a set of standards to differentiate superior wines from those that are merely good, and good wines from those that leave a lot to be desired.

More complicated yet, quality standards, especially in matters of taste, are highly subjective. That doesn't mean it's wrong to rate. But it does mean that a wine one person puts at the top of his or her list may seem only average to someone else.

Influential critics also have an impact on the price, availability, and ratings of many wines. Rave reviews tend to make limited-supply wines sell quickly at high prices—partly a reflection of the fact that lots of people want to buy wines that are rated #1. What's more, when an influential critic who likes a particular style of wine consistently ranks wines made in that style at the top of the list, some producers may modify their approach to produce wine resembling the ones getting the rave reviews.

US RATING SYSTEMS
There are four basic approaches to rating wine in the US, though there's no official system.

Verbal systems depend on words. A wine might be described as exceptional, very good, good, drinkable, or unacceptable. Other raters may simply describe wines as either recommended or not recommended. While describing a wine as "not recommended" sends a fairly clear message, saying a wine is good delivers a somewhat ambiguous message.

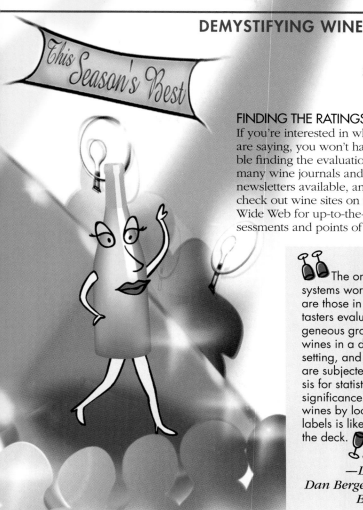

FINDING THE RATINGS

If you're interested in what the critics are saying, you won't have any trouble finding the evaluations. There are many wine journals and critics' newsletters available, and you can check out wine sites on the World Wide Web for up-to-the-minute assessments and points of view.

> The only rating systems worth trusting are those in which the tasters evaluate homogeneous groupings of wines in a double-blind setting, and the results are subjected to analysis for statistical significance. Evaluating wines by looking at labels is like stacking the deck.
>
> —*Dan Berger*
> *Dan Berger's Vintage*
> *Experiences*

Visual systems use stars or other symbols, assigning the greatest number of symbols to the highest rated wines. But you need to know how many levels are being distinguished and know how many wines fall into each category for the system to tell you anything.

The department of Viticulture and Enology at the University of California at Davis developed a comprehensive **20-point system** to provide a consistent basis for evaluating different elements of a wine. But the Davis system has been modified by wine critics and writers, so you can't be certain, when a wine is assigned a certain point value, whether the judgment reflects the original values established at Davis or some variation. For example, in some versions an 18-20 translates as outstanding, and in others as exceptional.

Perhaps the best known and most widely quoted wine ratings are based on **100-point systems**—though in fact the lowest score a wine can receive is usually 50. The appeal of these systems is that they're easy to understand—a 95 is a 95, after all—and can be a convenient way to think about how one wine stacks up against another. And you might get a kick out of testing your impressions against what professionals think.

On the downside, each different 100–point system uses different criteria, without specific point values for any of the components of a wine tasting (how it looks, smells, and so on). Because the judgments are subjective, the same wine often gets rated quite differently.

A Wine Tasting Glossary

BALANCE
When a wine's flavors, texture, and bouquet are integrated, so that no one element overpowers the others, the wine has balance. You can describe a wine that's not balanced with words like sour, flabby, sharp, or angular.

COMPLEXITY
A wine has complexity if its bouquet, flavors, texture, and finish combine to please you at many levels at the same time—as you sniff it, sip it, taste it, and swallow it. Wines lacking complexity are simple, neutral, or hollow.

BOUQUET
In a general sense, bouquet describes the way a wine smells. But more specifically, bouquet describes the more subtle and integrated effect that fermentation and aging create out of a wine's original aromas.

DEPTH
Depth describes wine flavors that are complex and rich. A wine that lacks depth can be described as flat, lean, or thin.

FINISH
A wine's finish is the impression of flavor you experience after you swallow. Finish is strongly affected by your sense of smell, triggered by the olfactory receptors near the back of your throat.

BUYER BEWARE
Unscrupulous wine merchants occasionally create a fictitious score—or jigger a mediocre one—to display with bottles they want to push, hoping that you and other buyers will pick up a bottle or two.

FORWARD FRUIT

When the first and most prominent flavors in a wine are simple fruits, and there's none of the complexity and range of flavors you find in a more complete or complex wine, you describe the way it tastes as forward fruit.

LEGS

The slow, beautiful dripping that occurs when wine is swirled in a glass and slides down the sides is described as legs. Surface tension created along the glass' wall by alcohol and glycerin in the wine produces the legs.

VISCOUS

A wine that looks and tastes rich, deep, and concentrated is often described as viscous. It's the opposite of a wine you might describe as steely or austere.

LENGTH

Length is the amount of time a wine's flavors linger in your mouth after you swallow. Longer is better, as long as the finish is pleasant.

PALATE

The way a wine tastes and the impressions it makes while it is in your mouth are its palate. Since you have a palate—the roof of your mouth—and the palate is also used to mean a sense of taste, it's easy to get confused when you hear the term used.

NOSE

The way a wine smells, and the components of its bouquet, are both known as its nose.

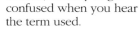

RESTRAINED

When a wine's bouquet or flavors give the impression of being held back, you can describe the wine as restrained. Think of it as a rose bud, in contrast to a fully opened flower.

Wine Bottles

You find traditional bottle shapes and colors around the winemaking world.

Though there are a few exceptions to prove the rule, the shapes and colors of wine bottles are striking most of all for their similarity.

There are three classic shapes for still wines, and one for sparkling wine. And there are three basic colors—though there are several shades of the most common color, green.

CLASSIC SHAPES

Because the traditional bottle shapes originated in Europe, they're still identified with European names.

Bordeaux. The distinctive, high-shouldered bottle has a long, slender neck. The shoulders are designed to catch the sediment produced as the classic red wines of Bordeaux age, and the neck to accommodate the long corks winemakers prefer if they believe a wine will age well.

Winemakers in other parts of the world traditionally use this bottle shape for cabernet sauvignon, merlot, Bordeaux-style blends, and often zinfandel, Chianti, sangiovese and other full-bodied reds. The same shape is also used for the classic white wines of Bordeaux—both sweet and dry—and worldwide for sauvignon blanc, sémillon, pinot grigio, and other crisp white wines.

Some US winemakers use a variation of the shape, more slender and an inch or so taller for cabernet sauvignons and Bordeaux-style blends.

Burgundy. The slope-shouldered bottle, sometimes slightly shorter than the classic Bordeaux bottle, is traditionally associated with the wines of Burgundy, the most famous of which

Chateau Lafite began aging red wine with the vintage of 1797. According to Alexis Lichine, that's when bottles were round enough to store on their sides.

BORDEAUX

BURGUNDY

are reds made from pinot noir grapes and whites from chardonnay grapes. So it's hardly surprising that, elsewhere in the world, it's generally the shape of choice for pinot noirs and chardonnays.

A similarly shaped bottled, sometimes embossed with a crest or other insignia, is often used in the Rhone region of France for red wines such as Chateauneuf-du-Pape and Hermitage, and for whites such as Condrieu. In Italy, it's often used for Barolo and Barabaresco wines.

Hock. The tall, narrower bottles used in the Alsace region of France and in Germany, where most of the wines are white, are called flutes in Alsace but are generically known as hock bottles because the English called Rhine wine hock. The only red wine you'll find in this shaped bottle is pinot noir from Alsace.

Leather containers popular in the late middle ages were known as "black jacks."

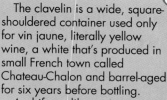

THEIR OWN DRUMMER

There are some wines that are always bottled in unusual containers.

The bocksbeutel, or boxbeutel, is a flat, oval-shaped bottle used for wine made in Franken, or Franconia (a region in Germany), in Styria (a region in Austria), and occasionally in other places such as Portugal and Chile.

The clavelin is a wide, square-shouldered container used only for vin jaune, literally yellow wine, a white that's produced in small French town called Chateau-Chalon and barrel-aged for six years before bottling.

And if you like variety, you can find wine bottles in many different shapes and colors, often developed for marketing purposes.

In other parts of the world, wine-makers use bottles of this shape, sometimes in a slightly different shape for rieslings, gewürztraminers, some rosés, and for wines they describe as German-style.

Champagne. Champagne bottles and the bottles used for other sparkling wines are also slope-shouldered, but broader and heavier than Burgundy-style bottles, to help withstand the pressure that results from the second fermentation in the bottle.

A LIMITED PALATE

Almost all red wine everywhere in the world is put into green bottles, though the shade may vary from quite light to very dark. The darker the green, the more effectively it blocks ultraviolet light, which can be harmful to wine.

Many still white whites are bottled in green bottles, as are most sparkling wines. Some white wine bottles and some sparkling wine bottles are clear, and others are the distinctive brown, or amber, of some German wines and wines made in that style.

Rosés are often put into clear bottles, making it easy to appreciate the range of tones and shades grouped into the category "pink."

PUNT!

One way that bottles do vary is whether or not they have a punt, the distinctive conical indention in the bottom of the bottle.

Champagne bottles always have a deep punt because it makes the glass stronger and better able to withstand interior pressure. The exaggerated indentation also allows the bottles to be stacked end to end during the fermentation process, prior to riddling.

Some Burgundy- and Bordeaux-shaped bottles

have punts, sometimes known as kicks or kick-ups. Punts aren't essential for still wines, though they make it more difficult for sediment to cling to bottom of the bottle.

Sommeliers and other servers sometimes make good use of the punt as a place to put their thumb while they pour wine, helping them to hold the bottle steady.

Sizing Up a Bottle

Wine bottles come in more sizes than they do shapes.

Traditional wine bottles hold 750 milliliters, which is 25.36 ounces, or slightly more than three-quarters of a quart. But you can buy bottles of still or sparking wine that hold as little as 187.5 milliliters—6.34 ounces.

If your needs run in the other direction, you can buy a six–liter bottle of still wine called an imperial. That's the equivalent of eight regular bottles. And you may find bottles larger than that. And if you need lots of Champagne, you can buy a Nebuchadnezzar, which holds 20 regular bottles, or slightly more than four gallons.

WHY SIZE MATTERS

The size of a bottle may influence the rate at which the wine ages. The smaller the bottle, the faster the process goes. The relationship is not directly proportional, though. For example, it doesn't take a magnum twice as long to age as it takes a regular size bottle, even though it holds twice as much wine.

Some experts maintain that the magnum is the perfect size for premium quality red wines that are expected to improve over time. That's because there's less exposed surface area in relation to the amount of wine

in the bottle. Others disagree, arguing that comparative tastings don't support the theory.

STILL PRETTY BIG

If you're buying large bottles of still wines, you need a slightly different vocabulary than the one you use to buy sparkling wine. The three-liter bottle, the equivalent of four regular bottles, is called a double magnum, not a Jeroboam. A Jeroboam of still wine is usually five liters in the US, though it may be four and a half liters elsewhere in the world, the same as a Rehoboam of sparkling wine. An imperial of still wine is six liters, the same size as a Methuselah of sparkling wine.

JEROBOAM
4 BOTTLES
3 LITERS

MAGNUM
2 BOTTLES
1.5 LITERS

BOTTLE
750 milliliters

HALF BOTTLE
375 milliliters

SPLIT
¼ **BOTTLE**
187.5 milliliters

BIBLICAL FIGURES

While the reasons for the names for large wine bottles remain obscure, the references are curiously Biblical.

Jeroboam: a king of Israel

Rehoboam: a son of King Solomon

Methuselah: the oldest man in the Bible

Salmanazar: a variation of Shalmaneser, a king of Assyria

Balthazar: one of the Magi

Nebuchadnezzar: King of Babylon who destroyed Jerusalem in the 6th century BC

A NEW LOOK

The most recent change in the way wine bottles look—with a flange rather than straight top—evolved as producers replaced lead capsules with a composite of aluminum and plastic, or a medallion sealed with beeswax or a biodegradable glue.

Thinking that one innovation deserved another, they developed the wider top. It actually resembles a much older bottle style, where the bottle's mouth was created when glassblowers used tongs to cut molten glass.

Using the new style is very much a matter of taste, however, with some producers using it extensively and some not at all. There's similar difference of opinion about whether the flange bottle eliminates the problem of drips. Some say yes. Others aren't persuaded that's the case.

NEBUCHADNEZZAR
20 BOTTLES
15 LITERS

BALTHAZAR
16 BOTTLES
12 LITERS

SALMANAZAR
12 BOTTLES
9 LITERS

METHUSELAH
8 BOTTLES
6 LITERS

REHOBOAM
6 BOTTLES
4.5 LITERS

30"
27.5"
25"
23"
21"
18.5"
14.5"
12.5"
10"
8"

Of all of the accoutrements of wine, none says more about its history than the development of the wine bottle. Prior to the 1800s, wines—even Champagne—were typically drunk very young and didn't leave the barrel until the day they were consumed. So, the primary purpose of bottles was to bring wine up from the cellar and to be a vessel that would not tip over on the table. The shape of the bottles reflected this. They were short and dumpy, and incapable of being laid down on their side. As the 1800s progressed, and the virtues of aging wine were revealed, the wine bottle evolved to serve a far more important use: long-term cellaring. Quickly, the bottle changed shape, becoming taller and longer, with straighter sides—the perfect shape for horizontal stacking in bins.

—*Emanuel Berk*
The Rare Wine Company

Under the Spreading Cork Oak Tree

There's more to a cork than the pop.

A cork has two important jobs: It keeps wine in the bottle and it keeps air out.

Corks aren't the only way to seal bottles. A quick glance at a grocery store's shelves reveals a variety of caps and screwtops designed to keep liquid in and air out. What's more, natural corks have their limitations. They can dry out and crumble, they can break, they can leak, and they can get infected with bacteria and harbor fungus (which is why they are chemically washed and dusted with sulphur dioxide).

But because of their long history as a sign of quality wine, and because most of them do the job they're designed to do—by expanding once they are inserted in a bottle and adhering snugly to the glass walls—natural corks are the stoppers of choice around the winemaking world. In fact, virtually the only wines available in screw-top bottles are very low–priced blends.

BARKING UP THE RIGHT TREE
Natural corks are made from the bark of cork oak trees (*Quercus suber*), which are cultivated primarily in Portugal. The trees must be about a foot in diameter—roughly 20 years old—before the inner bark can be harvested, or peeled off, for the first time. But it is bark from the third and subsequent harvests—18 to 20 years later—that is used for wine corks.

The panels of harvested cork go through several cycles of boiling, drying, and sorting before they are

> The best of the synthetic corks, which are made from food-grade foamed plastics, extract easily from the bottle with a normal corkscrew, don't crumble or break, and allow bottles to be shipped and stored with the neck up.
>
> —*Stuart Yaniger*
> *Neocork*

> **DOING DETECTIVE WORK**
> If the name of the winery and the vintage of the wine are stamped on the cork, examining them will tell you if they match the wine's label. But you're extremely unlikely to uncover a fraud.

sliced into strips about as wide as a wine cork is long—1¼" to 2". Then corks are punched out, some mechanically and others by hand, by skilled craftsmen. These are used in premium wines.

Then the corks are rinsed, washed in a chemical solution, rinsed again to neutralize the chemicals, and dried again. After being graded into one of six quality classes, they're sometimes treated with paraffin or silicon to make them easier to insert into a bottle, and given a small dusting of sulphur dioxide to help prevent spoilage.

As the demand for corks increases, there are concerns that the quality may decline, as trees are harvested further down the trunk, or when they are younger. Among the solutions may be amalgam corks made by pressing pieces of natural cork together to form the traditional shape or the recyclable polymer, silicon, or plastic substitutes that look almost like natural corks.

SNIFFING AROUND
Ceremonious homage to the cork—smelling it, caressing it, and presenting it with a flourish—has a following in some serving circles. But there's not much you can learn by smelling a cork that can help you evaluate a wine's quality. Even a crumbly, dry cork or one with mold on the top is no clear indication that the wine has spoiled.

Corks may get this kind of attention because some spoiled wines are described as corked or corky. The musty,

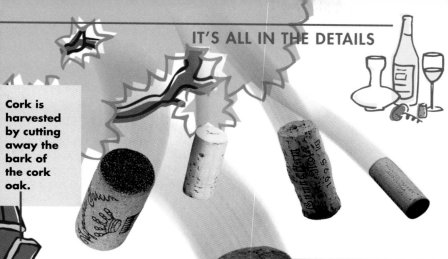

Cork is harvested by cutting away the bark of the cork oak.

damp smell of the wine is, in fact, caused by an infection in the cork, or by the chemicals used to clean it. If the wine is corked, or tainted, it will smell like wet cardboard.

WHAT CORKS CAN TELL YOU

Though the way a cork smells doesn't tell you much about the wine inside, the way it looks and feels may tell you that something is amiss. You'll have to taste the wine to know for sure, since none of these clues is proof of a fatal flaw.

If the cork is mushy and soft, it probably wasn't of high quality to begin with. That means the bottle may not have been tightly sealed.

If the cork crumbles and falls apart, it may simply be very old or it may have had a hidden defect when it was produced.

If the cork breaks, it may have dried out from being stored upright rather than horizontally or it may have gotten brittle because it was of poor quality.

If the entire cork is stained or wet, it may mean the bottle wasn't sealed tightly. In most cases, the stain or moisture should be no higher than

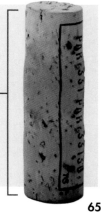

MUSHROOMING CORKS

How do the corks in sparkling wine bottles end up with their distinctive mushroom shapes? In fact, wine makers start with corks that are just a little fatter than the ones that go into still wine bottles. They insert the cork half way, cover the top with a metal cap and give it a whack to put it in place. As that happens, the pressure in the bottle exerts an upward force that distorts the cork, spreading it over the top of the opening.

two-thirds of the length of the cork and in younger wines even lower.

If a cork is defective, and air has gotten into the wine, the aging process will have speeded up and the wine may be oxidized. That means it may no longer be good to drink. The tell-tale clues are an aroma and flavor that seem stale or cooked rather than fresh or lively and a lower than normal fill level, which suggests leakage and evaporation.

CORK IT

You're more likely to find longer corks—approximately 2"—in Bordeaux bottles that winemakers expect to have a long life. The more standard length, used in the majority of bottles, is 1¼" or 1¾".

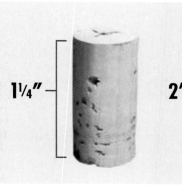

1¼"

2"

ut with the Cork

DOUBLE LEVER OR BUTTERFLY

DIRECT PULL

ASSISTED DIRECT PULL

WAITER'S

It's easy to get the job done if you have the right tools.

If you've never thought much about corkscrews, they may all seem pretty much alike. Most of them will get the job done—that is, let you get the cork out of the bottle. But some are easier to use than others, and some make the task far more fun.

There are hundreds of variations on three basic types of corkscrews—those that require you to pull, those that use leverage to make pulling easier, and those where you need only to keep turning the handle—sometimes called self-pullers.

TAKE A PULL
The most basic corkscrew, the **direct pull**, has three elements: the worm—the distinctively twisted piece of metal that's the screw in corkscrew—the shank, and the handle.

The most common direct pull is T-shaped, with a fixed, straight handle perpendicular to the shank. Other versions, which work on the same principle, have a loop handles, which vary from simple oval to the elegant ergonomic eyebrow.

When you use a direct pull, you twist the metal worm clockwise into the cork, which provides a grip as well as breaking the pressure seal between the neck of the bottle and the cork. Then you pull up with the handle. Given the resilience of corks and the effectiveness of modern techniques for inserting them, extracting a cork with a straight pull may require a force of several hundred pounds. A good comparison might be the power it takes to loosen the nut on a car tire.

HELP WITH THE PULL
There are some more sophisticated versions of the direct pull, called **assisted pulls**. They have an additional piece, typically a disk or an inverted bell, on the shank to limit how far the worm goes into the cork and provide some leverage. If you continue to turn the handle once the screw is in place and the extra piece is in position, the cork comes mostly out of the bottle, making the final pull easier.

GET SOME LEVERAGE
If pulling doesn't work for you, try leverage.

The best-known **single lever** corkscrew, called the waiter's corkscrew, differs from a direct pull by having a short arm of metal about two inches long hinged to the handle. After you insert the worm into the cork, you position the end of the short arm against the rim

COMPOUND LEVER

TWO PRONG

SCREWPULL

pulls the cork up through the mouth of the bottle.

Compound lever corkscrews, which are more common in Europe than the US, are typically constructed of hinged arms of metal that look like lattice work when they are open. You insert the worm with the arms closed, touching each other, until the cap rests on the top of the bottle. As you pull up on the handle, the arms spread apart, exerting pressure on the bottle, and pulling the cork out.

MAXIMUM TORQUE

Other styles, also called self-pullers, extract the cork from the bottle as you turn their handles. The best-known version is the basic Screwpull®. The worm is positioned within a plastic frame or cylinder about the length of the cork. You put the frame or the cylinder over the bottle top and turn the handle to insert the worm. When the worm is in place, you continue to turn the handle further, which lifts the cork out of the bottle.

DESIGNER MODELS

Some fancy corkscrews include wire cutters, a small brush for whisking away cork particles, or even jiggers, bar spoons, champagne knives, bottle openers and a host of other bells and whistles. You can decide for yourself how useful these gadgets are.

The lever model is a more sophisticated and expensive version of the original Screwpull. You place the device over the top of the bottle, pull the lever down so the worm penetrates the cork, and then pull up to extract the cork. Moving the lever to the open position again after the cork is out of the bottle releases it from the worm.

A TWO PRONG ATTACK

One corkscrew you either love or hate isn't a corkscrew at all, but a corkpull that's sometimes referred to as an Ah-so®. To use it, you wedge the two flat metal prongs, long prong first, down between the cork and the bottle, with one prong on either side of the cork, until they're fully inserted. Then you twist slowly, pulling the handle to extract the cork.

Inserting the prongs takes practice, since the space is tight. It usually helps to rock the device gently back and forth in what you might describe as a seesaw motion while pressing gently but firmly downward.

But if the cork is slightly loose, the corkpull doesn't always work. You may even risk pushing the cork into the bottle.

of the bottle and pull up on the handle. The leverage created by forcing the short arm against the rim makes the pulling action far less strenuous.

Double lever corkscrews, with their distinctive wings, are often described as butterflies. As you turn the handle to insert the worm into the cork, the wings lift up until they are almost perpendicular to the shaft. As you force the wings down, the leverage

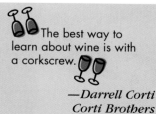

The best way to learn about wine is with a corkscrew.

—*Darrell Corti*
Corti Brothers

The Trick with Corks

You don't always need pull to extract a cork.

With so much choice, at such reasonable prices, you should have no trouble finding a corkscrew—or several—that work for you. If you ask around, you'll find some people who use just one style, sometimes a corkscrew they've owned for years, and others who use different devices on different occasions.

In fact, each type of corkscrew has its advocates and its detractors—sometimes passionate ones—but the truth is, practically any version can get the job done. And the process takes just a few seconds.

FIRST THINGS FIRST

There's one step in opening a bottle of wine that comes before using a corkscrew. You have to remove part or all of the capsule that covers the top of the bottle.

The easiest approach, and the one most restaurants use, is to use a simple foil cutter, a small plastic device with a sharp inside edge that, when you rotate it, cuts out a circle over the cork so you can insert the worm. Alternatively, you can use a sharp knife to cut around the covering at the top of the bottle's neck, just below the rim, and remove that top portion. Or you can simply pull off the entire capsule.

Dealing with corkscrews may require a little practice, but you don't have to be a magician.

> For 30 years, I taught wine appreciation at UCLA Extension. Humbly, perhaps not so humbly, I believed I knew all there was to know about wine until I met the corkscrew! It's the grape's greatest humbler!
>
> —*Nathan Chroman*
> *Author and Wine critic*

THE WAY THE CORK CRUMBLES

No matter how good you are with a corkscrew, you may encounter an occasional problem opening wine. But most of these snafus have fairly easy solutions. Sometimes, it pays to have a couple of different styles of corkscrews on hand.

- If you consistently have a problem getting the worm centered, switch to a corkscrew, such as the assisted pull or Screwpull®, that centers it for you, or try the corkpull version where no worm is involved
- If a cork breaks while you're taking it out, you can probably remove what's left in the bottle with a waiter's corkscrew, which gives you lots of leverage. If that doesn't work, or you don't have one handy, you can push the piece that's left into the bottle. Be careful though, as some wine

will probably splash upward as you push down
- If the cork crumbles, which can happen if it's dry, or old, or the bottle has been stored standing up for a long period, you may make out better using a two-pronged corkpull, which leaves the cork intact

NO CORKSCREWS NEED APPLY

You have some alternatives if you hate corkscrews, but they may not all be equally appealing.

One solution is to drink only sparkling wine as long as you're careful not to shake or agitate the bottle. You don't need a corkscrew—in fact you can't use one. Instead, holding the bottle at a 45° angle, with your hand firmly over the top of the bottle and the cork pointed away from you, you loosen and remove the wire that holds the cork in place. Then, holding onto the cork with one hand, turn the bottle with the other. That way, you can control the speed at which the cork is pushed out by the pressure in the bottle. The slower that happens, the better.

If you control the escaping carbonation, the wine won't spill and the cork won't fly across the room, potentially injuring someone or something. Nor will you lose the lovely mousse.

CORK ON THE LOOSE

The best way to get rid of any little pieces of cork that might be left in the bottle is to pour a small amount of wine quickly into a glass and dump it out, cork and all. Since cork floats, it should come out of the bottle first. And if some ends up in your glass, just scoop it out with a teaspoon.

Decanters Galore

Decanters are a happy marriage of form and function.

While you often decant wine for practical reasons, you get the added benefit of being able to serve your guests from a beautiful decanter. Whether you prefer a traditional design or one that's more sleek and modern, you should have no trouble finding a style to suit your taste and your pocketbook. Decanters are generally designed to hold a single bottle of wine, but some hold a magnum's worth. And smaller ones are ideal for storing what's left in a bottle after you finish dinner.

TRADITIONAL

The most traditional wine decanters are upright, the neck narrower than the base. The wider the area that holds the wine, the greater the surface that is exposed to air.

The clearer and less adorned a decanter, the more easily you can see and appreciate the color of the wine.

LEAD CRYSTAL
decanters bring a beautiful sparkle to wine service.

THE HORIZONTAL DUCK DECANTER
adds some whimsy to the table.

FULL STOPPER

Some decanters are fitted with snugly fitting stoppers, so you can store wine you don't finish. Keep in mind, though, you should keep the container in a cool, dark place, such as the refrigerator, and drink the wine within a few days. Even in a well-stopped decanter, most wines decline quickly in quality once they're opened.

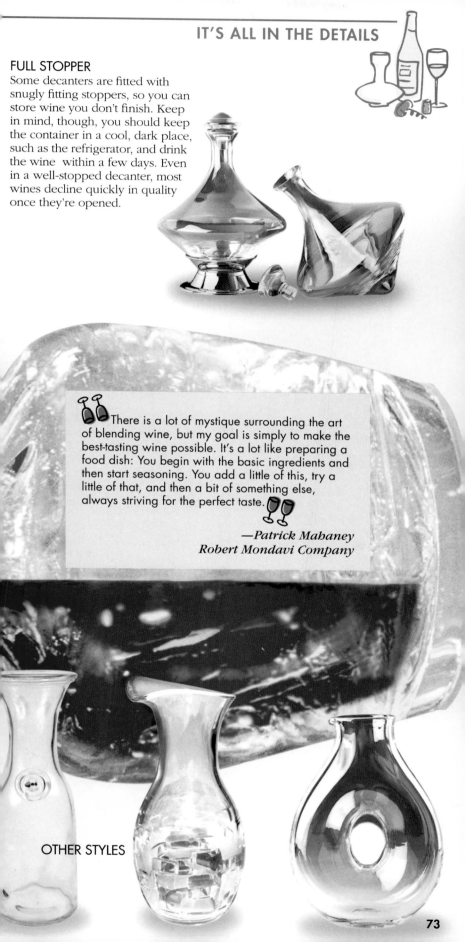

There is a lot of mystique surrounding the art of blending wine, but my goal is simply to make the best-tasting wine possible. It's a lot like preparing a food dish: You begin with the basic ingredients and then start seasoning. You add a little of this, try a little of that, and then a bit of something else, always striving for the perfect taste.

—*Patrick Mahaney*
Robert Mondavi Company

OTHER STYLES

Raise a Glass

You can drink wine from any glass, but that doesn't make it a wine glass.

Being able to choose the wine glasses you'll drink from is part of the pleasure of drinking wine. But there are so many options—from different manufacturers, in different styles, at different prices—it's hard to known where to start.

THE ESSENTIAL WINE GLASS

As different as wine glasses are, they all share some basic characteristics:

- The essential feature is a plain, transparent bowl, which is oval—sometimes described as egg-shaped or tulip-shaped—rather than square or rectangular
- The bowl balances on a slender stem, usually also plain and transparent, and long enough so that you can hold the glass by the stem, without having to hold the bowl
- The stem rests on a circular base broad enough to balance the glass

RIM

TRANSPARENT BOWL

STEM

BASE

MAKING CHOICES

If you have unlimited space and lots of money to spend, you can buy glasses in many shapes and sizes that cost from less than a dollar a glass to $100 or more.

A lot of serious research and years of trial and error have demonstrated conclusively that the size and shape of the glass you drink from, and the material from which it is made, influence your perception of a wine's aromas and flavors. If the glass is the right shape for the wine, the wine tastes better.

But the reality is that you often have room for a limited

number of glasses, a factor it's hard to get around even if your budget is flexible. So what do you do?

If you're tight on space or money, choose one all-purpose style—sometimes described as an AP glass—and use it for both red and white. Given a choice of sizes, larger is better than smaller.

If you've got a little more flexibility, choose one style for white wines and another for reds, buying an equal number of each. A slightly larger glass for red, with a somewhat wider opening is usually the major difference. That's because you may pour a little more red than white and may want to inhale the aroma a bit more deeply. If you serve rosé, use the white wine glasses.

You may want to choose separate glasses for sparkling wine. The classic flutes are longer and narrower that other wine glasses, to concentrate the wine's distinctive mousse.

HOUSEHOLD ISSUES

You can wash wine glasses by hand or in the dishwasher, if you can stand them up. Just be careful not to use too much detergent, or a rinsing agent, to avoid leaving a residue that could affect the taste of the wine you serve next. In fact, some experts suggest skipping the detergent altogether and taking the glasses out as soon as the rinse cycle ends.

ALL PURPOSE (AP)

If the glasses are very fragile or delicate, however, it's probably smart to wash them by hand. One way to help protect them from breaking in the sink is to layer the basin with a dishtowel and wash only one at a time. Let them drain on a paper towel placed over a dish towel, and then dry them with a linen cloth.

IN THE CLOSET

You can store your glasses upright in an enclosed cupboard, or invert them using a rack designed to hold them by their stems. Either way, the bowls are exposed to the air. That way, no stale odors, which could potentially taint the bouquet and flavors of the wine you serve, are trapped in the glass.

A MATTER OF TASTE

Some wine drinkers prefer glasses with cut and polished rims to those with rolled rims. You can tell the difference by running your finger up the side of the bowl. If the rim is rolled, you'll feel a bump— sometimes a very slight one—as your finger hits the top. But other people argue that the way the rim is finished makes no difference in the way the wine tastes.

WHY SHAPE MATTERS

If you've heard about the importance of using the right glass, you may be interested in why it matters. Here's part of the reason:

As you pour wine into a glass, it begins to evaporate. As the aromatic vapors rise off the surface of the wine, they fill the glass in layers determined by their varying densities. Once they have separated from one another, the layers do not blend back together, even as you swirl the glass.

The heaviest aromas, those of alcohol and wood, remain at the bottom of the glass, while the medium-weighted aromas, including those described as earthy and as green or herbaceous, rise to the center of glass. The delicate elements of fruit and flowers are on the top layer.

The shape of the glass determines the degree to which your nose and tongue are aware of each layer. That's why a light, fragile wine with fruit and flower aromas is best served in a tall, slender glass that brings the top layers of bouquet closer to your nose and tongue. In contrast, a bold red with woody flavors should be served in a glass with a larger, rounder bowl that gives more exposure to the bottom, heavier aroma layers. This allows you to sniff through the layers of the bouquet, from the lightest to the heaviest, fully experiencing the different elements of the wine.

Much of this research, and the design of distinctive glasses for different wines is the work of the Riedel Crystal company, which produces many shapes and styles for different wines in many price ranges.

AROMA LAYERS

WHITE

RED

SPARKLING

The Wine Tool Kit

Wine can be an equipment-intensive pleasure.

While all you really need to enjoy a wine is a bottle, a corkscrew, and a glass, you can find lots of other wine-related equipment in shops and catalogs.

Some of these tools may strike your fancy, or turn out to be the perfect gift for a wine aficionado. And even if you don't put them to practical use, they can be conversation pieces at the dinner table.

POURING SPOUT
You either love or hate pouring spouts, but they do the job they're designed to do. Spouts help you pour wine without dripping it on the tablecloth or on your guests.

FOIL CUTTER
A foil cutter simplifies the task of removing the capsule covering the top of the wine bottle. Just position the cutter at the bottle's rim, give it a quick turn, and you're ready to insert the cork.

TO FILTER OR NOT TO FILTER
Should you pour an older wine you're decanting through a filter? Some people consider it not only unnecessary, but unwise. They argue that it may remove too much of the wine's natural flavor. Advocates of filtering describe it as a way to be comfortable that the wine will be free of sediment.

CHAMPAGNE STOPPER

AIR-TIGHT STOPPER
An air-tight stopper helps you preserve the quality of a wine by letting you pump the air out of the partially finished bottle.

STOPPERS
Reusable bottle stoppers serve a practical purpose when you want to store a bottle of wine you haven't finished. The stopper's cork fits snugly in the neck, but it's easy to pull out.

BASKET

A decanting basket holds a bottle of wine horizontal and helps you keep it steady. But be sure to hold onto the bottle as well as the basket as you pour.

CORK RETRIEVER

If you're determined to retrieve a cork that has slipped into a bottle of wine, the cork retriever may be just the tool for you. You'll need patience to corral the cork and pull it out of the bottle.

CHILLERS

Chillers in all shapes and sizes are designed to keep bottles of wine cold after you've opened them. Or you can quickly chill a bottle that's not cold enough if you fill the chiller with equal parts of ice and cold water.

NO DRIP COLLAR

Slipping a felt-lined collar over a wine bottle's neck can help eliminate a drip of wine in the wrong place. Collars come in all styles, from sedate to whimsical, and in all price ranges.

The first preservation device I used (and sold) was a bag of clear marbles. You dropped them into the bottle to raise the wine level. The only problem was getting them back out of the bottle in order to clean them.

—*Ray Wolkoff*
The Flask Liquor

Wining Out

Ordering wine may seem like a major hurdle, but it doesn't have to be.

If your first reaction to a wine list is panic—even minor panic—think about this: The hardest part of the job has already been done by the person who selected the wines and put the list together. All you have to do is decide what to order.

In fact, picking the wine is actually a lot like choosing the food you want to eat from the restaurant's menu. Everything may sound comfortable and familiar, or most of the choices may be new to you.

When it comes to food, you sometimes make out best when you order the menu's specials or a dish the server recommends. The same can be true with wine, especially in a restaurant that offers a range of wines at different prices. The reason is the same: It's in the restaurant's best interest to have you enjoy your meal.

What if you order a wine you don't like?

Chalk it up to experience. It's no different from ordering a main course you don't enjoy. But if either the food or wine is spoiled, send it back.

What do you do with a wine list the length of a book?

Concentrate first on the type of wine you're planning to order and on the wines in your price range.

What should you expect to spend for a bottle of wine?

As a rule of thumb, plan on about the same amount as you're spending for one person's meal.

When we put our wine list together, we include a broad range of styles, prices, and levels of complexity in each varietal. We want all of our customers—whatever their tastes and level of sophistication—to have plenty of choices.

—*Laura Cunningham*
The French Laundry

How much should you order?

A good rule of thumb is that you'll need half a bottle per person at dinner, often less at lunch or if you've had a cocktail first.

What if you don't recognize the wines on the list?

Tell your server what you enjoy and ask for some suggestions, or take a chance on a name that strikes your fancy.

Putting it Together

There is a method in organizing a wine list, even if it might feel like madness.

Believe it or not, most wine lists are put together to make choosing a wine easier. To do that, wines that share one or more characteristics are typically grouped together and presented in a separate section.

Though you might encounter a list organized in a way you've never seen before, most lists divide first by color—into red, white and rosé—and sometimes add sections for sparkling wines and dessert wines. A wine list may be further subdivided by country or region of origin, by price, or by varietal. Typically, the longer the list, the more levels of differentiation there are.

THE COLOR PALATE

It's the unusual wine list that doesn't separate wines into red and white and into sparkling and still. They're not only the most obvious distinction, but ones that can help you zero in on your choice more easily.

If you're at all uncomfortable about ordering wine, you might (and maybe should) make a decision between red and white before you even look at the list. After all, if you're ordering only a white (or a red), you don't have to give the other part of the list a second thought.

Some lists make additional distinctions within color, identifying some reds as light-bodied while others are identified as full-bodied. That's one way the restaurant can give you some guidance about wines you may not recognize by name.

For example, if a wine you've had and liked appears in a section labeled light-bodied reds, you could stick with what you know—or you could try something new by choosing a different wine from the same group.

THE BOTTOM LINE

Price is often a factor in choosing a wine, sometimes the overriding one. And price can also be one of the primary organizing principles of a wine list. When that's the case, the usual approach is to list the least expensive wines first within each category, whether color, region, or varietal—though you may also find the reverse, with the most expensive presented first.

You can set a price limit in your head and concentrate on the parts of the list with wines in your price range. You can almost always find a wine you'll be pleased with at a price you are comfortable paying.

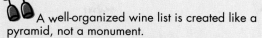

A well-organized wine list is created like a pyramid, not a monument.

- The top—high-end, collectible, and extremely rare wines—can be built high and thin
- The middle—excellent wines from highly regarded producers—must be balanced and inviting
- The base—moderately priced, high quality, and generally enjoyable wines—must be broad and interesting

—Piero Selvaggio
Valentino Restaurant

White Wines

A SENSE OF PLACE

Wines from different countries, different regions of a country, and different vineyards within a region have distinctive characteristics. Many wine lists group their selections by country, and sometimes by region, to make it easier for you to find the type of wine you're looking for. That's a boon—provided you know what you want. But what if you're not sure of the difference between Italian reds and Spanish reds, or Long Island chardonnays and California chardonnays?

Or what happens if you find yourself in a restaurant whose wine list is as focused as its food—exclusively Italian, exclusively French, or exclusively Chilean, for example—and you don't know enough about those wines to be comfortable ordering?

If there's someone at the table with you who's knowledgeable, ask for suggestions. You'd do that if the menu included food that was new to you, so why not do the same with the wine? And ask the server, just as you might inquire about his or her favorite dishes on the menu or which special is tastiest.

If you know the type of wine you want, say a light-bodied red or a fruity white, you can begin by asking which of the wines on the list are in that category. Or ask which wines are the most popular.

French

VARIETAL VARIETY

Within sections of a wine list organized by color or place of origin, you may also find that wines are grouped by varietal. For example, in a list of California reds, you may find a half-dozen zinfandels from different producers listed together. Or you may find chardonnays produced in a half-dozen countries in the same section.

Like other methods of organization, this approach can have real advantages if you know the varietals you like. While a California chardonnay may be very different from a South Australian chardonnay, the two will have more in common than a chardonnay and a riesling from the same region—or even the same vineyard.

*W*ine List Anatomy

A well-constructed wine list has a wealth of detail.

The more information you have about the wines a restaurant has available, the easier your choice should be. So it's worth taking some time to understand what the details on the wine list tell you.

While there probably won't be a "Best Buy" checkmark next to any of the entries, you can learn how to home in on a choice that will suit you.

ADDING INFORMATION

You may discover that some wine lists include the grape variety in the descriptions of some European wines—identifying sangiovese as the grape in a wine whose name is a place in Tuscany, a region of Italy. Though you won't find the varietal name on the wine's label when the bottle arrives, finding a name you recognize on the wine list can give you more confidence when you choose.

On the other hand, you may find geographic names for US wines that may suggest a particular origin—Napa Ridge, for example—but don't actually say where the wine is from.

The **bin number**, when used, indicates the wine's cellar location. Bin storage makes it easy for the server to locate the bottle—and it can be a convenient way to order if you're uncertain or uncomfortable about how to pronounce a wine's name. There are some tongue-twisters, like gewürztraminer or Pouilly-Fuissé.

The **wine producer**, generally the winery, which may be a family name or a place name, or both, and the **winery location**.

Faux's

Sparkling Wines

101 N.V. Neil Brut $
     Napa Valley

102 N.V. Mellisima Rosé
     Napa Valley

103 1990 Dom Fantasique
     Eperney   1/2 bot

White Wine

150 1996 Prom Dr Jugen Spätle
     Mosel

151 1994 DeWond Chardonnay
     Sonoma Valley

152 1996 Mavis Sauvignon Bla
     New Zealand

153 1995 Chateau Bliss
     Graves

154 1995 Domaine La Fleur M
     Montrachet

You can create a wonderful wine list with fewer than 100 selections that includes the stalwarts—sparkling, light and robust reds and whites, rosés—and some unusual choices. But you have to choose carefully.

—*David Fink*
Salish Lodge and Spa

A specific **vineyard** or cuvée is designated, when it applies, since it often identifies a wine that merits special attention. The same varietal from different vineyards, even when they're from the same wine-maker and vintage, can be strikingly different.

The **vintage**, or the year the grapes were harvested, should always be included. The exceptions are non-vintage (N.V.) sparkling wines, like the two here, and wines sold by the carafe or glass. Different vintages of the same wine might be available at very different prices, for many reasons.

The **variety**, or type of grape from which the wine is made, should be listed when applicable. In this list, the wines from California and New Zealand identify the variety but the French and German wines, for example, do not. In those cases, custom and law dictate that naming the grape is not necessary and the wines are known only by the region and producer's name.

Prices are shown for the regular 750 ml bottle—about 25 ounces—and for other sizes if they are available. Sometimes certain wines are also available by the glass, and that price will be shown, too. If you have a choice between a glass of unidentified chardonnay and a glass poured from a bottle on the wine list, the second is usually tastier and worth an experiment.

Faux's

Red Wine

200	1992 Domaine Shelby Pinot Noir Alexander Valley	$26 glass $6	
		$34	
201	1990 DeLox Merlot Nottingham Vineyard Spring Mountain		
202	1985 DeLox Cabernet Sauvignon Spring Mountain	$45	
		$175	
203	1975 Domaine Romalee Cotes Nuit		
		$275 $650	
204	1949 Chateau Courtenay Margaux 1.5L		

32

$65

$150

🍷🍷 Even those of us who are "experts" in the field see wines we don't know almost every time we look at a wine list. So, we ask a lot of questions. 🍷🍷

—*Beth Novak Milliken*
Spottswoode Vineyard
and Winery

The Sommelier

Tastevin

A serious wine list often comes with an expert to explain it and make some recommendations.

Does the prospect of a conversation with a sommelier, sometimes called the wine steward, give you indigestion? Like many people, you might find the experience intimidating, as any encounter can be if it's with someone you regard as an expert. After all, nothing can make you feel quite as dumb as listening to someone who knows a subject inside and out. But if your solution is to avoid the sommelier at all costs, you may be missing out on helpful advice and, if you're interested, the chance to taste a wine you wouldn't otherwise have ordered.

The sommelier is not an ogre...

If sommeliers intimidate customers, they are not doing their job. A sommelier should be a friend, not an adversary. We need to debunk the mythology of wine as a snob exercise.

—*Larry Stone*
Rubicon

He must think I'm a novice! This wine list is so long! What wine goes with all our dinner orders?

WHAT'S IN A NAME?

Part of your reaction to working with a sommelier may be in the name itself. It looks hard to pronounce (it's sum-mel-yay), so it seems designed to trap you into revealing you've never heard anyone actually say the word out loud. It may give you a different perspective to know that in French, sommelier means wine waiter.

On the other hand, the name conveys a sense of expertise and experience that shouldn't be taken lightly. A sommelier not only knows what's available, but what each wine tastes like. That knowledge, and practice explaining what those tastes are, can help take some of the tension out of choosing and ordering.

Typically, he or she will have sampled all the menu items as well, including the day's specials, reviewing their ingredients and style as part of getting ready for the meal. While a sommelier would be the first to agree that there's no one right wine to drink with any meal, the point of being an expert is to be able to identify a number of wines that, depending on individual taste, seem exactly right to people who drink them.

SPOTTING THE SOMMELIER

The way sommeliers dress and whether or not they wear a **tastevin**—the distinctive device used for sipping a small amount of the wine you ordered before pouring some for you to taste—generally depends on the formality of the restaurant and his or her personal style. But you don't have to worry about picking the right person out of a sea of tuxedos, or whatever the staff is wearing. Sommeliers introduce themselves to you.

SHOULD YOU ASK FOR ADVICE?

If you know exactly what you want, your only interaction with a sommelier may be to give your order and approve the selection when it's brought to your table. In fact, in many restaurants if you

comparable one. Or, if you recognize a wine from a highly regarded producer that's from a difficult vintage, you might ask frankly about whether it is worth the money.

PERSONALIZED SERVICE

One part of the sommelier's job, for which there's no parallel in food service, is that he or she tries to get an accurate sense of your taste in wine as well as the food you're ordering before suggesting a particular bottle. Part of being able to make a recommendation is based on asking for information—such as the tastes you enjoy, the varietals or wine-producing areas you know, and what you want to spend—and then knowing how to interpret the answers to help you make the right selection.

WHAT'S IN A JOB?

Helping you to choose a wine, delivering it to the table, and serving it during the meal, is only part of the sommelier's job description. He or she typically has a major role in creating the wine list, buying the wines, overseeing the storage, and supervising the way the wine is served.

Because a sommelier can't be at every table

...but a wine expert whose job is to help you choose a wine and serve it.

They clearly know good wine. How much do they want to spend? They should try Bin 43. It'll go with their meals.

don't ask specifically to speak to the sommelier, your server may handle both your food and wine orders.

But if you want help in choosing a special wine, or you'd like an opinion on a choice you're considering, or don't recognize many of the wines on the list, you can ask your server if you could talk to someone familiar with the wines that are available.

And if you're interested in wine, and want to learn more, a sommelier can help satisfy your appetite for knowledge as well as your appetite for food and wine. For example, you might describe a wine you really enjoyed and ask the sommelier to recommend a

and help every customer, especially when the restaurant is busy, he or she needs a wait staff that's also skilled at helping you choose wines you'll enjoy.

To provide that backup, many sommeliers develop training programs for the servers and sometimes the kitchen staff as well, covering everything from matching of flavors and textures to proper presentation and service. The instruction typically includes tastings—sometimes open and sometimes blind—discussions about what's being added to the wine list, and the foods those new choices might be paired happily with.

*M*aking Your Selection

So what's the wine going to be tonight?

You may know more about wine from one country than about wine from others, or at least feel more confident about how to choose. You may prefer one varietal to another—liking pinot noir better than cabernet sauvignon, for example. Or you may know you like the wine of a particular region, or even of a particular winery.

If you're just starting to order on your own, you may want to look for wines that meet those criteria. Then, as you grow more confident, you may want to experiment with a wine you've seen mentioned in a magazine or newspaper or one that's featured as the evening's special.

Your sense of adventure may grow stronger, too, if you're ordering with a group of friends or if you're by yourself and aren't worried about pleasing other people.

> ❝ We want to intrigue our customers with the selections on our wine list as well as give them their money's worth. ❞
>
> —*Cidy Correa*
> *La Toque*

WORKING WITH YOUR SERVER

But what if there's nothing on the wine list that rings a bell? It may happen that there's not a single wine you recognize, especially if the wine list is relatively short or it's been developed to complement an unusual menu or a restaurant that specializes in a particular cuisine. Or you may find that the wines in your price range are ones you don't know.

One solution is to ask your server's advice, or talk to the restaurant's host or owner. You may be surprised at how much easier it can be to choose a wine if you have guidance from someone who sees the list every day, and knows what other people are ordering and what they've liked. You may even find the conversation is one of the highlights of the evening—educational and enjoyable at the same time.

> 66 My favorite customers are the ones who are willing to try something new. 99
>
> *—Mark Jensen*
> *Marinus at Bernadus Lodge*

PINPOINTING YOUR CHOICES

Here some quick tips for asking advice from your server:

✓ Be as clear as you can about the kind of wine you want. The more direct you are, the more likely that you'll be happy with the wine your server suggests. Explain, for example, that you want a light-bodied red, not just a red, or that that you prefer a wine more like a Beaujolais than a cabernet. Or, if you like merlot, ask the server which of the ones on the list he or she would recommend, or which other wines are similar to a merlot.

✓ Be specific. Asking if the wine is fruity or crisp, or if it is more like a sauvignon blanc than a chardonnay, will probably produce a more useful answer than asking if the wine is a good choice.

✓ Be clear about the price range you're looking at. You can do it subtly by asking the server's help in choosing between two wines that cost about the same, or asking if there are other wines in the same price range that are worth considering.

✓ If the answers are vague, or if the server seems uncomfortable about giving advice, ask if there is someone else on the staff who can help you. The training servers get varies considerably, as does their comfort with wine. But there often is someone who can help.

DRINKING COMPANIONS

If you're ordering wine for yourself or for a dinner companion who shares your taste, you can move right to the section of the wine list that pleases both of you.

But if you're choosing for other people, you'll probably want to take their preferences into account. There are always ways to uncover different tastes without taking a vote, or making people feel uncomfortable. For example, you can ask what people's favorite wines are, or whether they've tasted the one you're thinking about ordering. Or you can simply ask if your guests would prefer red or white.

If some people express a preference for red and others for white, you can order a bottle of each.

If you're having wine before and with dinner, you might order one wine to start and another with the meal. Or, if some members of your party begin with a cocktail, those who prefer wine might each order a glass.

There may be a point when buying a bottle makes more economic sense. If each glass costs between $5 and $8, and two people have two glasses apiece, you'll spend a minimum of $20 and perhaps as much as $32—a range in which you'll probably find quite a selection of wine by the bottle.

On the other hand, for small groups choosing very different meals, wine by the glass throughout the dinner can be a smart choice. You can sample several different wines at the table without wasting or overindulging.

It's Your Call

One pleasure of ordering wine is that every list offers something different.

If one of your guests knows a lot about local wine, and you always enjoy the wine he or she chooses, it can be a nice touch to invite that person to make the selection. Or you might just want to ask for a suggestion or recommendation.

When splitting the bill, you might want to agree on the selection with your co-host. Or you might want to choose yourself, especially as you build more confidence. It's your call.

THE WINE OF THE COUNTRY

You can try new wines as you travel, as a way to expand your horizons.

If you're traveling in the US, you'll discover at least two interesting things about wine lists: Certain wines, especially a number of well-known labels from California, are available almost everywhere. If you like the chardonnay from a specific winery, for example, you can be confident you'll get the same wine whether you drink it in California, in Maine, or in Michigan.

But you'll often find an interesting selection of local wines, typically produced in the state or area you're visiting, and not available where you live. Since one of the best things about travel can be wining and dining on local specialties, it's almost always worth sipping a glass of local wine, or

ordering a bottle with dinner, as an experiment.

If you're staying in a local inn or small hotel, the hosts might offer you a taste of local wines to introduce you to the wineries in the region. The restaurants in the area may offer local wines by the glass, which can be a perfect match for regional dishes.

TRAVELING FURTHER AFIELD

Traveling to wine-making regions outside the US—France, Germany, Italy, Spain, Chile, Australia, and New Zealand, for example—also gives you an opportunity to taste delicious and often modestly priced wines you may have not had before. Experimenting helps you learn which wines you like best from the local selections. And there's no better way to practice a second language—or to have more fun—than to use it in the quest for a delicious bottle of wine.

You'll find that the skill you develop in reading a wine list at home can be a big plus almost everywhere in the world, even if you don't speak the language. Typically, the list will provide the same kinds of information on vintage, winemaker, and price that you're accustomed to. And you can always point to the one you want.

A BOTTLE OF YOUR OWN

One solution to the dilemma of wine selection is taking your own bottle to a restaurant. Realistically, though, it's a choice you're more likely to make if you want to drink a particular wine on a special occasion, or if the restaurant doesn't have a liquor license but lets you bring your own.

If the restaurant has a wine list, you may be charged a **corkage fee**, ranging up to $10 or more for each bottle, to cover the cost of glasses and service. Those amounts are built into the cost of the restaurant's wines.

The server should open the bottle at the table and pour you a small amount to taste. He or she should not assume that a wine you bring with you is necessarily drinkable, any more than one you ordered from the wine list.

In restaurants that allow wine but don't have a wine list, there may or may not be a corkage fee. Depending on the restaurant's policy—and possibly the server's whim or experience—your server may or may not open the bottle at the table and pour the first glass.

It's appropriate, if the restaurant does serve wine, to order a bottle from the restaurant's list to complement the one you bring. And it's a nice touch to offer the server, or the owner and the server both, an opportunity to taste the wine you've brought. In addition to being courteous, you're paying them a compliment by suggesting they'll appreciate your special bottle.

But here are a couple of caveats about taking your own bottle. It's not legal to take wine into a restaurant in every state or locality. And some restaurants simply don't allow the practice. It's smart to check first if you're not sure what their policy is, especially if you'll be embarrassed if they say no.

IF YOU'RE THE EXPERT

If you're asked to choose the wine by a friend who is hosting a restaurant meal, here are some things to keep in mind:

Consider your host's budget. Don't order a more expensive bottle than you normally would for yourself, unless you've volunteered to pay for the wine and your offer has been accepted.

Or you might prefer to offer a couple of differently priced selections and the reason you've selected each one. That way you're letting your host make the final decision.

Why are corkage fees criticized so often? Restaurants are one of the few businesses that let people bring their own entertainment. You can't sing onstage at a concert, juggle at the circus, or play your own instrument at the symphony. We even provide glasses, attentive service, and clean up after the guest has departed.

—*Michael Dellar*
The Lark Creek Inn

Clarifying Your Wine Order

Don't panic. If you can order an appetizer and main course, you can order a bottle of wine.

Are you one of those people who find actually giving the wine order the worst moment of the evening?

Worried that you'll pronounce something wrong?

Concerned that the server will look at you in scorn, fighting to hold back a withering look or a cutting comment?

Convinced they'll be out of what you order, so all your energy will be wasted and you'll have to start again?

Take heart. Help is here.

GETTING THE WORD OUT

The most typical way to order a wine is to ask for it by name, mentioning all the particulars—except the price. For example, if there are two vintages of the same wine, or two different vineyards of the same winery's or producer's varietal, be explicit. If it makes you feel better to point at the one you mean as you speak, do it. You'd do the same

when choosing among two very similar chicken dishes.

If you're afraid you'll trip over the name, and there's a bin number on the list, you can order by the bin number. Or try for some combination, like "I'll have number 151, the Chianti classico." Or do your best at the pronunciation and don't worry. Just take a stab, as you would ordering a new dish. You don't have to get it right. You can point to the right place on the list as you speak. The server will figure out what you want.

The one thing you don't want to do is pass up a wine you'd like to try because you're worried about how to say its name.

A MULTI-WINE MEAL

If you're ordering one wine to start the meal and another for the main course, you can order both at the same time. Or you can order the first bottle and hold onto the list and make the second decision later. Or you can ask for the list back.

Any way is fine, so you should do whichever is more comfortable.

An advantage of ordering at the same time is that then you can give your guests—and your wine—your full attention. An advantage of waiting to order the second bottle is giving yourself a bit more time to consider what you want. In other words, there are no fixed rules, and you should do what's comfortable for you.

When ordering two wines at the same time, a white and a red, for example, be sure the server understands when you want them opened and served. If you want your guests to be offered a choice of red or white from the start, make that clear. Similarly, if you've ordered the red for the main course, say so. And if the second wine is offered too soon, tell the server again when you want it served—ideally before any is poured.

NO SHOWS ON THE WINE LIST
It's frustrating to be told the restaurant is out of the wine you have chosen.

One solution is to go back to the drawing board, or, more precisely, to the wine list. If it's an informal occasion, you may even give the server two choices the second time around, so you won't have to look at the list a third time.

In fact, running out of a wine that's included in the list shouldn't happen

often, though it does occasionally, just as restaurants may run out of a popular dish before the end of the evening. Part of the problem is that many restaurants have very little cellar space, so they sell out a shipment before the replacement arrives. Also, some wines and some vintages are available only in limited quantities, and when they run out they can't be replaced.

Another factor is how frequently a restaurant's list is updated. If it's kept current, as the menu is, most of the wines will be available. That's one example of a happy mix of technology and wine service: Laser-printed lists make it possible and economical to update what's available every day.

Don't always assume that your server has mastered the wine names or can hear you clearly over the background noise in the restaurant, especially if you order a wine that may be difficult to pronounce. Pointing to your selection, and giving the bin number, can be a great help.

—Ned Kelly
Freelance Cafe and Wine Bar

One **bottle** for every two people

HOW MUCH WINE TO ORDER
The number of bottles you order depends on the number of people you're serving and how much is being consumed. You should plan on half a bottle per person over the course of a meal, since a bottle holds six to eight glasses, if poured to the appropriate fill level. If there are eight or more people at the table, it's usually smart to start with two bottles of the same wine.

The server, whose job it is to sell wine, will ask if you want additional bottles. That's your call. It's perfectly fine to say you don't want to order

more. And in a large group, you might have to tell the server explicitly not to open another bottle.

As the host, you should be alert to how much wine is being drunk, and when it's appropriate to reorder. If the wine is mostly gone, but you're very near the end of the meal, you might suggest that you're about to order more. If people have had their fill, they'll generally tell you, "No more for me, thanks," or "I'm fine, thanks," or words to that effect. Or you can simply make the decision yourself.

Presenting ... The Wine

It's hard to think of many rituals that have more fanfare.

There's no moment in a restaurant meal more enveloped in ritual than the time the wine is brought to the table—except maybe serving a flaming dessert. Here's what happens:

- The bottle is presented, sometimes with a flourish or a bow—or sometimes, with very little ceremony
- The cork is extracted, often with a waiter's corkscrew but sometimes with an elaborate device and much fanfare
- The cork is presented as if it were a valuable jewel or a sacred object
- The server pours. You taste. The wine is accepted, or worse, rejected
- Your guests take the first sip

It's hard to think of a moment as likely to provoke a sense of panic, or produce a knot in the pit of your stomach. After all, what seems to be on the line is your ability to choose a good wine. But once you're comfortable with ordering, this tension should disappear.

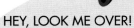

HEY, LOOK ME OVER!

The server's first job is showing you the bottle, to verify that it is what you ordered. To check, look first at the name and then at the vintage, the varietal, and the vineyard designation, if applicable. Also check for any other information from the wine list that made you select the bottle in the first place.

Call any errors or differences to your server's attention right away, the more specifically the better: "I ordered a 1994, not a 1995," makes the point much more clearly than "Is this what I ordered?"

Remember, though, that a vintage can—and does—get sold out, and is typically replaced with the next one. The list should be updated, but it may not always reflect the most current availability.

If the wine isn't what you ordered, you have several options, just as you would if the server brought your salad with blue cheese dressing when you'd ordered oil and vinegar.

- Accept the wine without further question

Better restaurants with serious wine programs will accept wine rejections without question. Our experience is that many are justified—though others are not. But we will always exchange the wine.

—*Robert Simon*
Bistro 45

- Accept the wine based on the server's assurance that this is an equal or better wine and they are out of your choice. Don't hesitate to ask if the substitute bottle is the same price as the one you ordered
- Reject the wine and accept the server's recommendation of a suitable substitution
- Reject the wine and substitute your second choice selection if you remember it
- Reject the wine, ask for the wine list, and start over

Any of these solutions is perfectly acceptable. Don't be intimidated or feel challenged. Do what seems most comfortable to you.

THE WAY THE CORK CRUMBLES

Once you accept the bottle—nothing more than a nod of your head or "Fine" is required—the server will pull the cork. This should be the least eventful part of the ritual, but occasionally, the cork may break or crumble for a variety of reasons.

An imperfect cork may or may not indicate a problem with the wine's quality. But you won't know for sure until you smell and taste. If the server offers to open another bottle to replace the first one, you can agree—or start by tasting the one that has already been opened. If it is good, there's no reason not to drink it. The cork itself is perfectly harmless.

To avoid errors, the server should double check the vintage, name, and vineyard before presenting the wine. If we are out of a specific selection, we let the customer know before bringing a replacement, so he or she can make the decision.

—*Celestino Drago*
Drago

CRUNCH TIME

The server will pour a small portion of wine for you (or the guest to whom you defer) to taste. If there's a flaw or defect, the smell or taste will reveal it. In that case, you have every right to reject the bottle, just as you would reject food that tasted spoiled or was badly prepared.

If you suspect a defect, but aren't sure, you may want one of your guests—ideally a knowledgeable one—for an opinion before you make the decision. (But it's probably not a good idea to ask everyone at the table to offer an opinion.)

Equally important, remember that wines are made in different styles. You shouldn't reject a wine simply because it's different from what you expected or you don't especially like it, but only if it is flawed.

HANDLING REJECTION (THE WINE'S, NOT YOURS)

If you reject the wine, you should explain as clearly as you can why it is unsatisfactory. The server will probably taste the wine and possibly ask the restaurateur or manager to taste it as well. This is common practice and certainly called for, so don't be intimidated. Remember, you're not on trial, the wine is.

If you're reasonable and reject wine only for defects, most servers and restaurateurs handle this rather delicate issue quite smoothly. Often they will suggest you order a different wine, or you may ask to do so. It may be a better decision than tasting another bottle of the same wine. Defects vary by bottle, so a second one may be fine, but the last thing anyone wants is a second bad bottle.

What if the server says the bottle is fine and doesn't take it from the table even if you ask? Chances are it won't happen. But if it does, be reasonable but insist that the bottle be removed. Don't be intimidated or embarrassed. There's never any reason to accept, drink, or pay for a wine that is bad.

Fill 'er ... Half Up!

Once the wine starts flowing, there's a way to keep it on course.

After you've tasted and accepted the wine, the server pours for your guest or guests first, and for you (or the taster you designated) last.

Keep in mind that no one's glass should ever be poured more than one third to a half full—even less if it's a large glass. Because a wine's **bouquet** is so closely tied to its taste, the larger the space and the longer distance it has to travel to get to your lips, the more you can enjoy the way it smells, and the more pleasure you will have anticipating its taste.

A CUP MAY RUN OVER, A WINE GLASS SHOULD NOT

Some servers tend to overfill wine glasses, either when they pour initially or as the meal goes along. While that practice increases the amount of wine ordered (which the restaurant may like), it rarely increases the pleasure of drinking it. And you may find yourself embarrassed or upset at having to deal with the consequences.

For example, what if the server pours the first few glasses so full that the bottle is empty before your glass is poured? Or what if he or she keeps adding wine to the glasses of people who are drinking very little? In either case, you'll probably have to order an additional bottle so that there will be enough to go around.

It's often easiest to say right from the start what you want. Before the server begins, say explicitly to pour only a small amount so the wine can breathe. If the first glass is poured too full, say so. You can even indicate the amount, or fill level, you prefer with your fingers. You might be hesitant,

especially if you're a little uncertain of yourself or don't want to be rude. But if you don't say something, you'll be angry at yourself later, especially if you feel the server took advantage of you.

In the same vein, if a server keeps refilling and overfilling, you may have to be more assertive, or offer—in a lighthanded way—to pour the wine yourself. Or ask that the bottle be left on the table so that people can help themselves. If the restaurant encourages its servers to push as much wine as possible, especially to larger groups, you may have to insist that the glasses not be overfilled. A smart server should get the picture with one pointed comment.

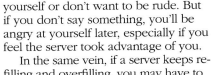

GLASS PIECES

Whether your table is already set with wine glasses, or they are brought to the table after you order the wine, the server should ask each guest if he or she would like wine rather than simply pouring wine into each glass.

It's also a good idea for the server to volunteer to remove glasses that aren't going to be used. That way wine doesn't get poured—and wasted—in error, and the person who has declined once doesn't have to keep saying no.

ATTENDING GLASSES

The server should bring new glasses for each different wine you order as a sign of good service. That's equally true whether you follow one white with another white, a white with a red, or a red with another red. If the server doesn't bring new glasses, don't hesitate to ask for them.

If you order a second bottle of the same wine, there's no reason to change glasses. But the new bottle should be presented to you, or the person you defer to, and a fresh glass provided for tasting. You should have the opportunity to approve the new bottle, since variation from bottle to bottle is possible, although generally this only occurs with older wines. Since you don't want to follow a delicious bottle with one that may be spoiled or doesn't measure up, be sure to taste again before the glasses are refilled.

There are some occasions when you may tell the server simply to pour additional bottles without your tasting each one. For example, if you order two bottles to begin, you may elect to taste only one. The same is true if, over

particular setting and what you're comfortable with.

Attentive service can be a pleasure if glasses are regularly refilled to the appropriate level as people drink the wine. But if you prefer to pour yourself, perhaps because you think it is more personal or intimate, don't hesitate to say so. The server should agree without an argument and leave the wine on the table rather than taking it to a serving station between refillings.

For a large group, the easiest solution may be to have several bottles on the table, so guests can pour for themselves or for each other. It's also an easy way to keep track of whether you need to order more.

STICK OR SWITCH?

If you've ordered a wine, and want a second bottle during the same course, should you stick with the one you're drinking or switch to a different one? It ought to come as no surprise that there's no right or wrong answer.

If you like what you ordered, you'll enjoy more of it. Or go ahead and try something different. The one drawback is that you'll have to look at the wine list again. The only rule is that if you are not happy with what you're drinking, don't order more.

RED   LARGE RED   PORT

the course of a long meal with a large number of guests, you order additional bottles of the same wine. But if you're more comfortable tasting every bottle that's brought to the table, by all means do it. The choice is always yours, and the decision should always be yours—not the server's.

CONTINUING SERVICE

Who should refill the glasses—you, your guests, or the server? In fact, all are appropriate depending on the

Overpouring wine is an ill-gotten concept of customer service. The best that can be said about it is that it's an attempt to make sure that the customer has a full glass. At its worst, overpouring is a deliberate effort to sell more wine.

—*Leonard Schwartz*
Maple Drive

Wine at Business Dinners

In choosing wines, as in running meetings, it pays to anticipate your audience, and have a good idea of the outcome.

If you're uneasy about ordering wine, having to make the selection for a business dinner can make you yearn for the return of Prohibition. But once you're comfortable with the basics of choosing and taking delivery, being the host at an important dinner can be a lot easier.

EARLY DECISIONS

A business dinner is rarely the place to experiment with a wine you don't know. Instead, focus on special wines you're familiar with that fit your price range.

It's probably not the ideal time to order the most expensive wines since they may not get the attention they deserve when there is work to be done, and they can drive the bill up quickly. In addition, older and often more expensive wines may not appeal to everyone,

> **Visit or fax the restaurant before hand!**
>
> **WINE INFO**

with the third lowest price. If your mind goes completely blank, you can try that.

Perhaps a smarter solution, especially if you're not familiar with the restaurant's wine list, is to visit the restaurant ahead of time or call and ask that the list be faxed to you. That gives you an opportunity to look it over, do a little research on the choices, and check to be sure that the wines you intend to order will be available.

> **Go with what you know!** OR **Try the 3rd cheapest.**

since their flavors and bouquets can be distinctive, and quite different from what your guests are familiar with.

Nor are business dinners the right time to order the least expensive wines. While they are often pleasant, being so obviously economical may not be in keeping with the tone you are trying to set. One approach that simplifies the process, but may or may not provide pleasing results, is always to choose the wine

The manager or sommelier will offer valuable advice, since they want you to be happy (and schedule more dinners). If you make your plans ahead of time, they may even ask you to come in for a tasting.

The other advantage of planning ahead is that you can settle matters like the amount you want to spend, the order in which wines will be served, and the number of bottles you want to begin with, just as you would if you pre-ordered the menu. The less you have to think about at the last minute, the more you can concentrate on your guests.

A LUNCH TIP

One way to handle the question of wine at lunch is to check with your guests before the server does. If a number say yes, you can order a bottle. If it's just one or two, you might each get a glass. One thing you may not want to do is to risk embarrassing a guest by not ordering a glass yourself after he or she has.

Ask a guest who is a wine expert to order.

THANK YOU!

EXPERT HELP

If one or more of your guests is a wine expert, it can be flattering to invite him or her to order the wine. You may even be able to learn something for your next dinner from the type of wine that is chosen.

Remember, though, that if someone other than you orders, that person should also taste and approve the wine.

However, you'll still want to make it clear to the server that you are the host, and that you will set the dinner's pace and also get the bill. If you're younger than the others or if you are a woman, the server (especially an inexperienced one) may assume that someone else is the host. That's most likely to happen at a small dinner that the server might mistake for a strictly social occasion. The best defense is to anticipate the mistake ahead of time and be ready to identify yourself.

If you're ordering for a large group, remember that a banquet room's wine list will usually be different from the main dining room's. Since you'll need more bottles, it's designed to give you more flexibility at lower cost. But it's also true that most restaurants have only limited quantities of the most sought-after wines.

—Christophe Granger
Sherwood Country Club

Make sure I know you are the host!

HELLO MY NAME IS: HOST

TALK TO ME

If you're concerned that you may not be recognized as the host, here are some hints to help you make it clear:

- Be sure to identify yourself to the restaurant's host or hostess as the person who made the reservation. Saying you expect your guests shortly should make your role clear as well. If the server's attention span seems short, you may want to be more assertive
- When you're shown to the table as a group, choose the seat you want, but stand until everyone else is seated
- Ask for the wine list. If it is being offered to someone else, say that you'll take it
- Order water for the table
- If someone else is ordering the wine, make it clear to the server that you've asked the person to do so

Handling Wine's Little Problems

Knowing how to deal can make life a lot easier.

As if choosing the wine for a meal and having it served the way you like isn't hard enough, there's the issue of what to do with the cork, whether you should have the wine chilled, and how to handle the inevitable tip question.

TIP, PLEASE

Getting the tip right—or what seems right to you—can be the most difficult decision of the meal, especially when the bill includes one or more bottles of wine.

You may wonder, for example, whether you tip the server separately for the cost of the wine or include it in the overall tip. You may not be sure whether you tip the same percentage on wine as you do on food. And you may be concerned about whether to tip the sommelier—if there is one—in addition to the normal tip for service. One of the problems is that in the US there are no rules on tipping, though there are some generally accepted norms. But even they vary from region to region.

One approach is to leave one tip to be shared by all of the serving staff, which works well in restaurants where tips are pooled and shared. Adding your customary percentage on the entire bill can be much easier than trying to decide who is entitled to what and figuring out how to distribute it in the manner you want.

AND ABOUT THE RATE

Most experts agree that it's appropriate to tip at your normal rate on the entire bill, including the wine, with one exception: You might leave a slightly smaller percentage when the wine is very expensive, and as a result, represents a disproportionate amount of the bill.

Following this model, on a bill for four that included two bottles of moderately priced wine—say each bottle cost about as much as one person's food bill—you'd tip your customary amount on the total. But if the two bottles cost significantly more than the food, you might reduce the bill in your head to what it would have been with a more conventional selection and tip on that amount.

If you bring your own wine, the opposite is true. If your server poured for you, you should increase your tip to cover the amount a bottle of wine would have cost you had you ordered one.

TWO WAYS TO TIP

1 One tip for all servers.

2 One tip for serving staff. Separate tip for the sommelier.

66 My job is to encourage customers to drink delicious, interesting wines that match well with our cuisine. Of course, I stand by any recommendation I make, and will not charge for any bottle if a customer is unhappy with it. 99

—*Michael Bonaccorsi*
Spago Beverly Hills

Finally, don't forget that if there are six or more in your group, many restaurants add a service charge to the bill. The rate—often between 15% and 20%—will be stated somewhere on the menu. You might want to leave a bit more if the service has been exceptional. But you'll kick yourself if you forget about the service charge and leave your customary percentage on top of that.

WHAT SOMMELIERS THINK
Sommeliers sometimes express the opinion that they should receive a separate tip for extraordinary service. What most sommeliers mean by exceptional service is not simply taking your order, which any server could do, but providing really helpful advice about food and wine pairings, delivering the wine you order to your table, and serving it attentively during the meal.

Among the things they don't always agree on, however, are
• What the appropriate percentage of the bill their tip should be
• Whether it should be in addition to the customary tip to the wait staff or a portion of that total
• How it should be indicated on a credit card receipt if there's no separate line for the sommelier or captain
• Whether it should be paid in cash
The bottom line: You have to handle tipping in a way that seems comfortable to you. If you're really pleased, you can tip more. If the service seemed perfunctory, your tip can be perfunctory as well. If there's no separate line for separate service, you can write one in. Or you might ask to speak to the sommelier after the meal and hand him or her the tip you want to leave in cash.

In fact, the gesture of recognizing the service may be more important than the amount of the tip.

TO CHILL OR NOT TO CHILL
If you order a white wine or a rosé, the server will probably ask if you want it chilled, or may simply assume that you do and bring an ice bucket to the table. Or, in some restaurants, after pouring the first round, he or she may take the bottle to a central serving station.

On the other hand, if you want the wine to warm up slightly, to bring out complex flavors and bouquet that may be muted by cold, you can simply ask that the bottle be left on the table. The server can still handle the pouring, if that's in keeping with the restaurant's style.

SOME BREATHING TIME
Since many fuller-bodied red wines, such as cabernet sauvignons, merlots, or zinfandels, taste better when they've had time to breathe, or mix with the air, you may ask your server to pour this type of wine when you order it, even if you plan to have it with your second course. That way, the wine will have had time to "open up" by the time you're ready to drink it.

You can explain what you're doing to your guests, if you're concerned that someone will be uncertain about which wine to drink when.

The Way It's Said

Who doesn't need a little help with pronunciation?

Here's a list of some of the words that could stand between you and feeling comfortable ordering a bottle of wine. Obviously, it only skims the surface of all the words you might see on a wine list. For example, it doesn't include the names of specific producers either in the US or overseas. And it deliberately omits words you'll probably never have to pronounce to order a bottle of wine—like *mis en bouteille au chateau* or *Erzeugerabfullung*, which, in French and in German, tell you a wine was estate-bottled. But it's a start.

REEZ ling

shah BLEE

KEY on tee

Barolo	bar oh low
Barbaresco	bar BAR es ko
Beaujolais	boh jhoe LAY
Beaune	bone
Bordeaux	BORE dough
Brut	brute
Burgundy	BUR gun dee
Cabernet	kah burr NAY
sauvignon	soh veen YOWN
Chablis	shah BLEE
Champagne	shahm PAIN
Chardonnay	shar dun NAY
Chateauneuf-	sha tohNUFF
du-Pape	dew-PAH
Chianti	KEY on tee
Clos	klo
Côte or côtes	coat
Gamay	gah MAY
Gavi	GAH vee
Gewürztraminer	ga VERTZ tra MEE ner
Graves	grahv
Gris	gree
Grenache	gren OSH

🍷🍷 I've worked with several unusual grapes that grow well in our cool climate. Their names (like Müller-Thurgau or Gewürztraminer) are neither glamorous nor romantic, but the wines pair so well with foods that they are worth the extra effort it takes to grow, vinify, and sell them. 🍷🍷

—*Susan Sokol Blosser*
Sokol Blosser Winery

mare SO

ree o HA

san GEE o VAI se

sir AH

Mâcon	may CON
Médoc	muh dock
Margaux	mar GO
Merlot	mare low
Mersault	mare SO
Méthode	may TUD
champenoise	shahm pen WAHZ
Noir	nwar
Nuits	nwee
Pinot grigio	PEE no GREEGE io
Pinot noir	PEE no NWHAR
Pomerol	palm muh roll
Pouilly fuissé	pooh yee fwee SAY
Pouilly fumé	pooh yee foo MAY
Riesling	REEZ ling
Rhone	rone
Rioja	ree o HA
Sancerre	sanz sear
Sangiovese	san GEE o VAI se
Sauternes	saw turn
Sauvignon	SOH veen yown
blanc	BLAHNK
Sémillon	sem y YAWN
Shiraz	sure AS
Soave	swa VAY
Syrah	sir AH
Village	vee lage
Vin	van
Viognier	vee ohn YAY
Vouvray	VOOV rey
Zinfandel	ZIN fan del

Wine at Home

The most interesting pair at the dinner table may just be the food and the wine.

Do you ever worry about how to choose wine when you're planning to entertain? Do you wonder whether you're serving the right wine with the menu you're preparing? If these nagging thoughts ever cross your mind, read on.

Like selecting wine in a restaurant, buying wine to serve at home involves developing a sense of what you like and learning how to make choices that please you—and your guests. At first it may seem even harder selecting what to drink at home, since nobody hands you a wine list from which to choose. But the truth is, you can create your own list of specific wines or types of wine that you enjoy and want to share with your guests.

And since you'll probably create that list through trial and error, think of all the fun you will have trying different bottles to find the ones you like and want to serve.

A RULE OF THUMB

How do you decide on the food you're going to serve when you entertain? Of course, part of the answer depends on the kind of entertaining you're doing: Inviting two or three people for a cookout on Friday night is a lot different from inviting a dozen for a more formal dinner on Saturday. And hosting the

The Chicken

When I think about pairing food and wine, sometimes I look for a contrasting choice and sometimes a compatible one. For example, a sweet Sauternes can be a perfect foil for a salty cheese, or it can be a match with orchard fruit.

—*Robert Houde*
Charlie Trotter's

family at Thanksgiving is different from wanting to impress your boss with an elegant brunch—or your favorite person with an intimate dinner.

Choosing wine is much the same. The occasion makes a difference in what you serve, and so do the people who will be drinking the wine with you. Just as you suit your menu to your guests' tastes, you'll probably want to serve wine that they, as well as you, will enjoy with the food you serve.

In fact, picking out wine is usually a lot easier and less complicated than preparing the meal. Shopping for one or two wines is quicker than shopping for all the food you need. You won't

suddenly discover you're out of a crucial ingredient. And there's virtually no preparation. Besides, since everyone will be eating the same thing, you don't have to worry about choosing an appropriate wine when one guest orders steak and another orders fish, as often happens in a restaurant.

THE CHICKEN OR THE EGG?

Do you plan the menu first and then choose the wines? Or do you chose a wine you like, and then plan a meal around it? Either works. But it's probably fair to say that most people decide on the food first, often because they are more comfortable with cooking (or putting together a meal of prepared food) than they are with choosing wine.

In fact, though, the process of choosing wine can be a lot like deciding on what food to serve. Do you sometimes try to recreate a dish you enjoyed in a restaurant or in someone's home? Have you ever tried something you watched being prepared on a television cooking show? Do you sometimes find a recipe in a cookbook or newspaper that sounds terrific?

You can try a similar approach for choosing wine. When you go to a wine store or the wine section of your supermarket, look for a name you recognize from having ordered it in a restaurant or being served it at a friend's house. It's no secret that one of the reasons winemakers like to see their wines on restaurant lists is that it's an ideal way to get people to recognize the name and ask for it in retail shops. And from your perspective, there's no better way to identify new wines you want to serve at home than to experiment when you eat out.

Also check out the food and wine columns in your newspaper or in magazines with features on entertaining as well as publications that focus directly on wine. You can get some great ideas, and if you try some of the suggestions, you'll discover rather quickly which food and wine writers consistently point you to tastes and combinations you enjoy. You might also visit some of the wine sites on the World Wide Web. The only real mistake you can make when you're entertaining at home is thinking you have to find the perfect wine to go with the meal.

When you're serving food and wine, try various combinations to find what pleases you. Enjoy the search, and don't be intimidated about experimenting. Since there aren't any absolute rules for pairings, you can't break them.

—*Erik Blauberg*
21 Club

Home, Sweet (or Dry) Home

Entertaining at home is a perfect time to experiment with new tastes…once you've tried them out.

One of the best reasons for entertaining at home is being able to share your enjoyment of delicious food and wine with friends and family. That doesn't mean entertaining has to break the bank. And you don't have to slave all day over a hot stove. But you probably do have to give some thought to the food you're going to serve and the wine you're going to drink.

GIVE IT A WHIRL

Try serving new wines as well as new foods. You might not want to experiment when your boss is coming to dinner, or if it's your turn to entertain difficult relatives. But you can have fun introducing friends and family to wines they haven't tasted before. And if you're lucky, they'll return the favor.

One way to expand your wine horizons and get new ideas about what to serve is to make a point of ordering something from a restaurant's wine list

that you haven't had before. Sticking with something you know might seem more comfortable, especially if choosing wine makes you nervous. But always drinking the same wine, like always ordering the same main course, can get awfully boring.

You might start your wine search by asking the sommelier or server for suggestions about what would be good with the food you're ordering, talk to them about their favorites, or ask if any bottles are new to the list. If you like what they recommend, write down the names or ask for the empty bottle.

When you go to your local wine store, buy several different wines of a type you know you like, and try them over the next week or so. Or buy a bottle or two of a varietal you don't know, or a producer you haven't heard of. If you find something you like, you can go back and buy enough to serve the next time you entertain.

It can be a real boon to find a wine shop with an interesting selection at different price levels. Introduce yourself to the owner. It could be the start of a long and satisfying relationship.

MY EXPERIMENT

CRITIC'S CHOICE

Wine Store Pick

The Usual

A PERSONAL TASTE LIBRARY

The goal of all this deliberate experimentation is finding a whole range of wines to enjoy and share—just as you pass along recommendations for movies or vacation spots that you've discovered.

Some types of wine—and some particular producers—may become favorites and the standard against which you make future comparisons. Some you may not particularly like, and choose not to serve again. And you might have a mixed reaction about still others, so that you may want to try them again with other foods or on other occasions.

As you taste more wines, you'll have a clearer sense of not only what you like, but why. That helps you describe what you're looking for when you go shopping for wine, and makes it easier for the wine merchant to make recommendations—just as it helps to be able to describe the kind of book you like to a book lover or librarian when you're looking for something new to read. In both cases, you're more likely to be happy with the results.

TASTE IT FIRST

Unless you have a death wish, a monster ego, or the world's most tolerant guests, you're probably not going to serve a menu you've never prepared before. Chances are you'll want to try it out first, or at the very least some of the dishes, on friends or family. Or, if your menu includes one dish that's new for you, you'll probably want to be sure you can make the rest of them in your sleep, or that they're easy to buy ready-made.

The same approach works with wine. Open a bottle of the wine you're planning to serve several days ahead—long enough to give you time to go back to the wine shop to buy as much as you'll need. Or, if you're not happy with it, you can choose something else. You don't want to be disappointed, or worse yet, embarrassed, by serving something you discover at the last moment to be mediocre, or something you don't like.

Remember, though, that people have different tastes in wine, as they do in food. Not everyone you're serving will love every wine—or every part of the menu either. You've probably been in that position as a guest yourself.

So it always pays to have some beverage alternatives available, just as you might be conscious of serving enough different dishes with a meat main course so that a vegetarian won't have to go home hungry.

IT'S IN YOUR COURT

If you want to experiment a little, try some of these food and wine pairings which you may not have thought of before:

Broth or Cream Soup	Dry Sherry
Foie Gras	Sauternes
Chocolate	Cabernet Sauvignon
Walnuts	Port

Happy Marriages

When it comes to food and wine, matches aren't made in heaven. They happen at the table.

Some wines bring out the flavors of certain food better than others. Similarly, some foods bring out the flavors of certain wines better than others.

While you'll find that nearly everyone agrees on some ideal matches, and there's a consensus on unhappy pairings, there's a large middle ground where you can create your own combinations to suit your own taste, as traditional or as unusual as they may be.

MOST FOODS CAN ... AND DO

Have you heard that you shouldn't serve a salad with a vinegar dressing because vinegar spoils the taste of wine? Or that wine is a poor choice with foods that are very sweet or very sour, like chocolate mousse or citrus salad? Or that wine and vegetables don't mix?

You may agree. But does that mean if you're serving broccoli, you should forget about wine? Or if your main

course is a spicy chili, you should only serve beer? Sure, if that's how you feel. But there are other solutions.

Chances are the offending vegetable fills only a small portion of the plate anyway—and that chicken or pasta or fish get center stage. For example, if there'll be chicken on the plate with the broccoli, choose a wine you enjoy with the chicken, whether it's white, red, or rosé.

If you start with a salad, serve it with a crisp white, such as sauvignon blanc. Or wait to serve wine until you get to the main course. If the salad follows the meal, your guests can continue to drink the wine you served with the main course if they like.

> I don't think about specific flavor matches—a wine that tastes like raspberries with a chicken dish that has raspberries in the sauce—but about blocks of flavor. If the food is rich, I choose a full-bodied wine. If it's delicate, I choose a lighter wine.
>
> —*Christopher Shipley*
> *21 Club*

A CLASSIC PROGRESSION

If you want to serve a traditional, some-what formal meal, you can choose wines to match the progression of courses, from appetizer through dessert. Modern meals rarely have more than three or four courses, even on the most elaborate occasions. So you might serve three or maybe four wines: perhaps a sparkling wine before the meal, a white wine with the first course, then a red with the main course, and perhaps a dessert wine to end.

Traditions about serving wine, like traditions in other areas, often evolve for good reasons. The reason many people serve a white before a red is that the white is usually more delicate, so it might seem pale by comparison if it followed a robust red. The same logic applies if you're serving two whites: In that case, you'd probably serve the more intensely flavored second. And if you were serving two reds, one lighter than the other, you'd offer the lighter one first.

By analogy, think about the order in which you'd prefer to eat the following foods:

Menu A	Menu B
roast chicken	grilled lamb
fruit tart	cold cucumber soup
smoked trout	baklava

Wouldn't you rather have the trout before chicken and the baklava after the lamb? That's the same reason you'd most likely enjoy a crisp sauvignon blanc before a buttery chardonnay or a light pinot noir before a rich cabernet sauvignon.

ONE WINE—OR SEVERAL

Do you need a different wine with every course? If the answer you'd like to hear is that you're under absolutely no obligation to serve more than one, you can relax. It's perfectly okay to serve the same wine from the start of a meal to its finish.

It can also be fun to serve several different wines, typically with different courses. And there's also no reason why you can't serve two wines with the same course if that's what you want to do. The more you experiment, the more you'll discover what you enjoy doing and what seems to work with a particular type of meal.

FRENCH FOOD...FRENCH WINE?

If your menu features food from a specific country or region, should the wine be from that region as well? If the point of the meal is really the region—a celebration of Bastille Day or Thanksgiving —you surely won't have any trouble finding wines to suit your theme.

But one of the great things about cooking at home is that you can create a delicious meal with nontraditional pairings, or one where the appetizer, main course, and dessert each owes its inspiration to a different cuisine.

So, can you serve a California wine with a French-inspired seafood stew or an Italian wine with a chili-crusted chicken? The answer is—but, of course!

Wine Inside!

If you enjoy drinking wine with your food, you'll also like eating food made with wine.

Pairing food and wine generally means choosing the wine to accompany a particular meal. But if you cook, pairing food and wine also means using wine as an ingredient in the food you prepare.

In fact, some dishes are so infused with wine that it forms their name: Coq au vin, beef bourguignon, and veal marsala are well-known examples.

LET ME COUNT THE WAYS

Like choosing the wine you drink with specific meals, cooking with wine can follow certain established traditions or be innovative and experimental—or both. What you should know is that different techniques produce different effects and serve different purposes.

One of the simplest is using wine—generally a rather small amount—to add distinctive flavor to a cold soup, sauce, or other un-cooked dish. The type of wine you choose depends on the other ingredients of the dish and the effect you want, though you'll find whites and sherries suggested most often in recipes.

Probably one of the best known culinary uses of wine is as an essential ingredient of a reduction, or quick-cooked sauce prepared just before serving, where it provides the distinctive flavor. Red, white, and sparkling wines are used in these preparations, as are fortified wines such as Marsala, Madeira, and Port. A related technique is using wine to degrease a sauté or

Choice ❶

Use the same wine for both serving and cooking

roasting pan, adding flavor to the liquid you serve to accompany the food.

Wine is also delicious in braised dishes, where the food is browned and then cooked slowly in liquid. Sometimes the wine—often red but sometimes white—is used alone, sometimes it is diluted with other ingredients. In each case, the wine helps to tenderize the dish and add flavor.

You can use wine as an ingredient in marinades to tenderize meat, chicken, or fish and create a distinctive flavor. The length of time the food marinates is important, so you may need to experiment to get the best results

TIPS FOR COOKS

- Choose full-bodied wines. Light, flowery, and fruity flavors tend to get lost when they are heated.
- Use an equal amount of stock or water when you cook with white wines, especially acidic ones.
- Don't substitute one wine for another randomly. For example, the sugar in sweet wines gets even more intense as it is cooked, so it produces different results from dry wines.
- Fortified wines are more intensely flavored than unfortified ones. Typically, two tablespoons of a fortified wine have the same flavoring strength as a half cup of red or white wine.

Wine is a great poaching liquid, too. You can poach chicken or fish, for example, in white or sparkling wine and then use the poaching liquid to make the accompanying sauce. Or you can poach fruit—pears in red wine is a classic—for an easy dessert.

And, if you tend toward the dramatic, you can use wine to flame food. It works best if you warm the wine before you ignite it.

A STEW ABOUT COOKING WINES

There's lots of debate—some of it heated—about whether the wine you use in preparing food should be the same one you serve with the dish.

On the one hand, wine that's been heated or combined with other ingredients doesn't taste the same as it does when you pour it out of the bottle. That's the argument for not using expensive or special wines in cooking. On the other hand, cooking concentrates a wine's flavor. Pleasing flavors become more intense, but so do unpleasant ones.

You can weigh these different points of view in deciding what to do:

- When you add wine to food at the end of the preparation, you should always use the wine you're serving
  - The wine you're cooking with doesn't have to be as special as the wine you're serving, but it should be similar or have similar characteristics
  - Any wine you cook with should be something you would enjoy drinking. Any wine that's not good enough to drink— that's vinegary, corky, or musty—will detract from the taste of the dish
  - It's fine to use up leftover wine in cooking as long as it has been stored in a cool place or refrigerated, and it hasn't been hanging around too long.

Choice 2

Use one wine for cooking and a similar wine for serving

REDUCTION

When you use the cooking technique known as reduction, you concentrate a liquid's flavor by reducing its volume. For example, if you bring a cup of wine to a boil and simmer it in an open pan for about ten minutes, what you'll have left is a much more intensely flavored quarter cup of wine. As you reduce the wine, you also cook away its alcoholic content, which volatilizes, or evaporates into the air.

Reduction is an essential step in creating wine-infused sauces. To get the most pronounced wine flavor, you reduce the wine separately and swirl or whisk it into the sauce after you remove the pan from the heat. Or, to get a more integrated result, you can add the wine to the sauce pan and reduce it, adding the other elements of the sauce and heating them together.

1 Pour 1 cup wine into the pan.

2 Heat. Reduction takes place.

3 Whisk the reduced wine into the sauce.

A Wine for Every Food

Whether you are a traditionalist or an iconoclast, food and wine are made for each other.

One myth you can uncork and forget about is that there is a right wine for a particular dish. It's true that lots of people think that a rich, garlicky pasta sauce works better with a red than with a white wine. But if you like white, you can find one you'll enjoy with almost any food. The same is true if you prefer red with fish or sparkling wine during the entire meal.

FOOD AND WINE ARE MADE FOR EACH OTHER

You can be a traditionalist when you pair food and wine, if you're happy with the custom that you always serve red wine with red meat and white wine with white meat. Or you can experiment a little with less typical food and wine combinations, pairing a red wine with Thanksgiving turkey, for example.

TRY THESE COMBINATIONS

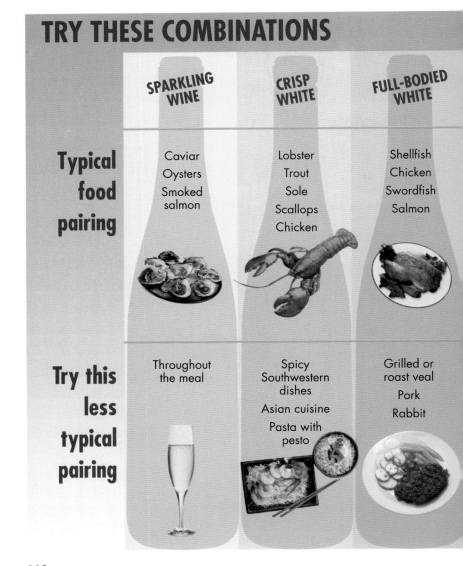

	SPARKLING WINE	CRISP WHITE	FULL-BODIED WHITE
Typical food pairing	Caviar Oysters Smoked salmon	Lobster Trout Sole Scallops Chicken	Shellfish Chicken Swordfish Salmon
Try this less typical pairing	Throughout the meal	Spicy Southwestern dishes Asian cuisine Pasta with pesto	Grilled or roast veal Pork Rabbit

> Red wine with seafood? Of course. We're civilized and open-minded. Besides, we don't make white wine.
>
> —*Art Finkelstein*
> *Judd's Hill Winery*

There's a lot you can learn from innovative chefs and sommeliers who work together to offer pairings based on textures or flavors rather than on color.

It's easy to try different combinations because you have so much choice, not only among producers making the same varietal, but among different varietals, including some that are being made from wines that in the past were used primarily in blends.

What's more, discussions of food and wine that are so evident in magazines and newspapers, on radio and television, and increasingly on the Internet, are a great source of ideas.

IT'S ALL ABOUT FUSION

One reason the old guidelines don't work as well anymore is that the food you eat isn't the same food your parents or your grandparents ate.

What's the traditional wine for French food with an Asian flair, for New England ingredients livened up with Southwestern spices, or for any of the other fusions you serve?

Experimenting is the only way to find an answer.

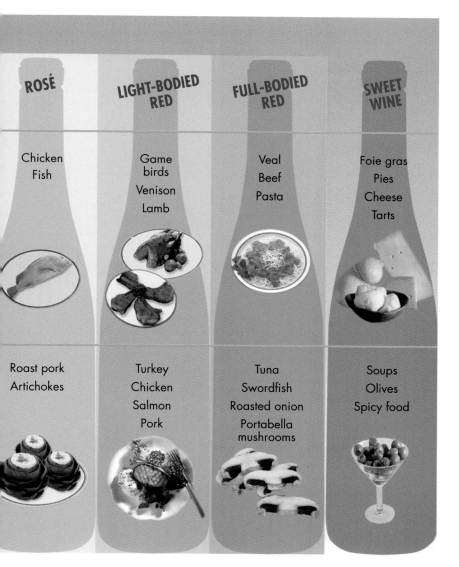

ROSÉ

Chicken
Fish

Roast pork
Artichokes

LIGHT-BODIED RED

Game birds
Venison
Lamb

Turkey
Chicken
Salmon
Pork

FULL-BODIED RED

Veal
Beef
Pasta

Tuna
Swordfish
Roasted onion
Portabella mushrooms

SWEET WINE

Foie gras
Pies
Cheese
Tarts

Soups
Olives
Spicy food

Delight in the Details

At party times, some wines, like guests, need to keep their cool.

You know who's coming to dinner. You've picked the menu, and you have an idea about the wine you want to serve. Now it's time to deal with some practical details.

HOW MUCH FOR HOW MANY

The amount of wine you'll need to buy and serve depends on a number of factors, which you can juggle a bit as you discover what works for you.

The most general guideline is that you need to count on about a half bot-

- You may need more wine if you're serving it with hors d'oeurves before the meal, or if the evening's entertainment is focused on food and wine. That's especially true if your guests won't be driving afterwards
- You may need more wine if you're serving several different wines, and your guests sample each one

RESERVE TROOPS

As you buy the wine you expect you'll need, remember that it's always smart

WHEN YOU NEED LESS

- **– LUNCH**
- **– BRUNCH**
- **– IF SERVING OTHER DRINKS**

WHEN YOU NEED MORE

- **+ SEVERAL COURSE MEAL**
- **+ DAY LONG EVENT**

tle per person when you serve wine with a meal, or the equivalent of about three or four glasses. But keep in mind:

- You'll probably need less if you're entertaining at brunch or lunch, since most people drink less in the middle of the day, and some won't have any wine at all. Also, there are typically fewer courses and a shorter time frame
- You'll probably need less wine with a single course meal than with one that has several courses, since people drink as they eat. Serving more food usually translates into the need for more wine
- You will probably need less wine if you're serving cocktails before the meal or if you're offering beer or other beverages in addition to wine as a choice with the meal

to have some in reserve. You don't want to be embarrassed by running out halfway through the meal, and you certainly don't want to feel pressured to open a special bottle you've put aside for a particular occasion—or one you know is mediocre—because you run short.

On the other hand, if you're serving a special wine with the appetizer, and a different wine with the main course,

👓 My favorite way to entertain is having four to six friends sharing wine and helping to prepare the food. There's nothing worse than being in the kitchen when your guests are enjoying themselves in the living room. 🍷🍷

—*Cal Stamenov*
Marinus at Bernardus Lodge

you don't need to plan for more than a glass or so per person of the first wine.

CHILLING THE WINE

Chilling enhances the delicate and crisp flavors of many wines, particularly sparkling wines, lighter whites, rosés, lighter Beaujolais, and dessert wines. So it's customary to serve those wines at colder temperatures. Serving them too warm can enhance the heat of the alcohol, overpowering the flavors, especially in the finish.

One cooling technique is to put the bottle in a bucket of half ice/half water for about 25 or 30 minutes. Another is to refrigerate it for a couple of hours. But don't put the bottle in the freezer, where it will get too cold too quickly, possibly damaging the wine and ruining its flavor and bouquet.

The flavors of other wines, especially fuller-bodied whites such as chardonnays, can be muted or repressed if they are served too cold. And reds—with the exception of light Beaujolais—are generally served at room temperature and not chilled at all. Their flavors and depth are masked when they're cold.

The bottom line is that personal preference plays a big part in deciding the temperatures at which you prefer to serve and drink certain wines. The more you experiment, the more quickly you'll figure out what you like.

SAVING OPENED BOTTLES

If you open a bottle you don't finish, what should you do? Once a bottle is opened, a rapid aging process begins, which means the wine will deteriorate.

To save the wine, first recork the bottle, since you want to slow down the aging process. Remember that a part-empty bottle will age faster than a full one, and a warm bottle will age faster than a cool one.

Always refrigerate opened whites, and either refrigerate opened reds or put them in a dark, cool place, such as a closet or basement. Before you drink a red wine you've stored in the refrigerator, take it out so it can warm to room temperature. You may find it's not as tasty as it was when you opened it the first time, since extreme cold can affect the taste even after the wine warms up.

If it is carefully recorked and cooled, opened wine can be good to drink for several days. If it goes off, you'll probably have to discard it.

WHICH ROOM TEMPERATURE?

The idea of serving wine at room temperature predates air conditioning and central heating. A more useful rule of thumb is to serve reds between 60° and 70° Fahrenheit—cooler than many rooms but not so cool the bottle is cold to touch.

Clink!

If you're serving wine, glasses are part of the story.

The more beautiful the glass, many wine drinkers believe, the greater the enjoyment of drinking wine.

And one of the pleasures of entertaining is that you get to choose the glasses as well as the wine you're serving in them. Whether you're buying your first set, or are ready to replace the ones you've been using, you'll find you have lots of choices, in all price ranges—just as you do with the wines you'll pour into them.

IT'S OKAY TO MIX

Don't worry about having separate glasses for each wine you're serving during a meal. You can serve them, one after the other, in the same glass. Just be sure each guest has taken the final swallow of the first wine before you pour the second. If he or she doesn't want to finish the first one, simply dump out what's left before you pour. You don't want to mix them in the glass.

Should you rinse the glasses between courses? It isn't necessary, and frankly it probably isn't practical to remove all the glasses, rinse them, drain them, and return them to the right places. Since in most cases you won't be moving from a red to a white wine, skipping the rinse won't affect the color either.

What's more, you don't want to use warm glasses. Heat volatilizes the alcohol, overpowering or distorting the flavors.

GLASSES ONE AND ALL

If you're choosing the wine glasses you're going to use from among a variety of different shapes and sizes, you can follow these helpful guidelines:

- If you have a choice between larger and smaller glasses, choose the larger ones, so you can enjoy the bouquet as well as the flavors
- If you have a choice between stemmed or stemless glasses, use those with the stems. If you hold the

glass by the stem you can avoid warming the wine to your body temperature (and there won't be fingerprints on the glass to cloud the appearance). But remember that in Italy, and in some Italian restaurants, wine is often served in small tumblers—a good example that when you're in Rome, you do as the Romans do

- If you have a choice between clear glasses and colored ones, choose the

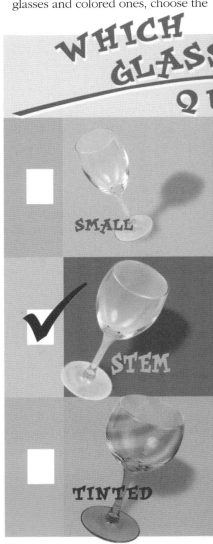

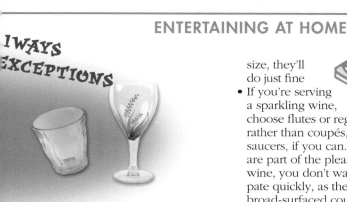

*IWAYS
XCEPTIONS*

clear ones because the color of the wine is part of the pleasure and you won't see it in a colored glass. But if colored glasses are what you have, by all means use them. They certainly won't stop you from enjoying the wine

• If you have separate glasses for red and white wine, and you have a choice of two or more sizes, use the larger ones for red. But if you have lots of glasses that are all the same

size, they'll do just fine

• If you're serving a sparkling wine, choose flutes or regular wine glasses rather than coupés, or shallow saucers, if you can. Since the bubbles are part of the pleasure of sparkling wine, you don't want them to dissipate quickly, as they will in the broad-surfaced coupés

ARRANGEMENTS

As with many other things you do in social settings, there's a customary way to position wine glasses at a place setting. It's the same pattern you use in arranging knives: The glass your guests will use first is farthest to the right, and the one they will use last—or at least the one that will be poured last—is farthest to the left, or the closest to the dinner fork.

If you'd prefer, you can also put new glasses on the table as you are about to serve a new wine, the way many restaurants do. That might work better if the table is small or seems likely to get crowded.

BEST?

BIG

NO STEM

CLEAR

BUFFET TIPS

If you're serving a buffet, you might want to simplify the wine service. As anyone who has tried carrying a wine glass in one hand and a full plate of food in the other will tell you, balancing them can be a real trick. A nice touch is to offer poured glasses of wine to your guests after they've found a seat.

Or, if guests are sitting at tables you've set with flatware and glasses, you could handle the wine service just as you would a sit-down dinner, either by pouring the wine for your guests or by putting bottles of wine on the tables.

115

Wine Is Served!

In choosing the wine, you're like a sommelier.
But as the host, you get to enjoy it too.

The conventions of wine service are the same at home as they are in a wine-savvy restaurant. Pour each glass a third to a half full—or less if the glasses are large—and pour a second round when glasses are getting close to empty. People drink at different rates, with some consuming very little. As you fill glasses throughout the meal, you can skip those people who are only sipping. If they want more, they'll have drunk more by the time you come around again.

It's also your call about how much to serve. For example, if you're almost ready to bring out the dessert, you may decide against opening another bottle of the wine you served with the main course. But if the conversation is lively, and you have another bottle in reserve, you might decide to open it. There's often a fine line between what's enough and what's more than you need, but it's a decision you should be comfortable making.

DON'T BE A DRIP

If you want to avoid dripping wine on your guests, the tablecloth, and maybe your own sleeve, there are some techniques you can learn early.

First, pour into a glass sitting firmly on the table. The margin for error is much greater if you're trying to hold the glass in one hand and the bottle in another. Even more dangerous is the bottle in your hand and the glass in someone else's.

As you finish pouring, lift the bottle gently, and rotate it slightly clockwise if you're right-handed, or slightly counter-clockwise if you're left-handed. It's an

> Doing food and wine pairings is a real trip. I love helping people find the treasure chest they carry around in their mouth and nose.
>
> —*Janet Trefethen*
> *Trefethen Vineyards*

> My idea of the perfect evening at home is experimenting with new dishes that pair with great wines.

TO TALK OR NOT TO TALK

In some settings, talk about the wine and the pairing of food and wine can be one of the pleasures of the meal. But in others, it may be unnecessary or even distracting. Depending on the mood of the party and who your guests are, you may want to explain what they're drinking, either as you begin to pour or after everyone is served. And you may want to say why you chose the particular wine you did.

easy, natural motion, and it works. The effect is that the bottle faces up and any potential drip is stopped in its tracks.

The more often you pour, the smoother and more graceful you'll be at doing it, so that it never seems like a fuss. You can practice with a wine bottle filled with water.

If you prefer, you can insert a spout into the bottle to help reduce drips as you pour. There are several versions available, although not everyone likes to use them.

You'll probably want to keep a towel or extra napkin handy to wipe off the bottles you're keeping chilled in a wine cooler. But don't wrap the towel around the bottle Hollywood waiter-style when you serve. It can get in your way, and make it more difficult to pour.

SELF SERVICE

You may want to pour the first glass of wine and then delegate the responsibility for keeping your guests' glasses appropriately filled, probably to someone you know well and whose approach will be similar to your own. That can make life easier for you if you're preparing and serving the meal yourself or helping your co-host prepare and deliver a number of different courses to the table.

You can also pour the first glass and then put the bottle (or bottles) on the table for people to help themselves. It's less formal, but also less work for you. And it can make people comfortable, as guests won't have to wait for more, or say no when you offer. This style works well, too, if the table is long or guests are seated at several tables.

ANOTHER RESPONSIBILITY

Ideally none of your guests, especially those who will be driving, will drink too much. Deciding how to handle the situation if that happens is never fun, but you can't simply ignore it either.

If one person has been drinking more than others, or is clearly intoxicated, you may simply decide to stop serving altogether and open no more bottles. That may be easier than refusing to serve a single individual who may have lost all inhibitions.

If nothing else, you should try to arrange for someone else to drive or encourage the person to take some other form of transportation. Should your guest be in an accident, your legal responsibility for any damage will be determined by the state or locality where the event occurs. But the possibility of a guest being injured or injuring others is probably not one you want to face.

But I always keep it simple so I can enjoy my company.

—Larry Levine, Monty's Steak and Seafood

It's Party Time

Getting the right wine for the right cost takes some planning, but pays off in the end.

Whether you frequently have big parties or you host one only occasionally, you want your guests to feel they've been included in a great event. And you want them to be eager for the next invitation. The wine you serve—and the way you serve it—can help make that happen.

Plan Ahead

Number of Guests + Bottles of Wine + Other Food and Beverages

$Budget

QUANTITY OR QUALITY?

You don't have to choose between quantity and quality when you serve wine at a party. Nor do you have to break the bank or blow your budget. But you'll want to spend some time planning and choosing.

The first step is to figure out how much wine you need. That will depend on who's coming, how long they're staying, and what else you're serving.

If you know everyone you're inviting (and how much they're likely to drink), or if you've given the same kind of party before, you may have all the experience you need to make a reliable estimate. If you'd feel better with a little guidance, the same rule of thumb—a half a bottle per person—works for a large party as well as a small one.

Remember, too, that it's usually smart to buy a few more bottles than you think you'll need.

Many wine shops will take back unopened bottles of wine that you've bought to have in reserve. But you may want to ask their policy before you buy. It may be illegal in the state or locality where you live, or it may be

> When I was a student in Croatia during World War II, and didn't have enough money for a full meal and wine, I would buy half a meal and a glass of wine. The wine made me feel I was having a full meal.
>
> —*Mike Grgich*
> *Grgich Hills Cellars*

118

a courtesy merchants extend only to their most frequent customers. If you can't return the extra bottles, don't worry. You can always find a time to enjoy them at a later date.

COSTING OUT THE WINE

Unless money is no object—in which case you can skip this section—you'll want to set a budget for wine, just as you set a budget for food, flowers, and the other costs you anticipate when you're hosting a party. If you work out what you're willing to spend ahead of time, just as you would if you were ordering wine in a restaurant, it will be easier to choose and you can be more relaxed about your selection.

The kind of party you're planning and the guests you're inviting are the things you'll want to think about most. For example, your wine budget for a neighborhood barbecue will probably be quite different from your budget for a more formal dinner party—even if you've invited the same number of people.

Does that mean you don't spend as much on wine for the barbecue? It may mean you don't have to. The type of wine that might be perfect for an informal occasion—perhaps a young zinfandel—may be less expensive than a more complex chardonnay, cabernet sauvignon, or Burgundy you choose to complement a more formal menu.

Or, you might discover you actually budget the same total amount for two different parties, more bottles of less expensive wine for an informal party and fewer bottles of more expensive wine for a more formal one.

KEEPING TO YOUR BUDGET

What do you do if you're not sure what a realistic budget might be, or how to anticipate the cost of the wine? Once you've estimated the number of bottles you'll need, multiply that number by the price you paid for the last bottle of wine you enjoyed (remembering to use the wine store price, not the price you paid in a restaurant). If that total seems like an amount you're willing to spend, all you have left to do is buy the wine.

An alternative is to set a limit on the total amount or the amount per bottle you're prepared to spend. You can find good wine in a wide variety of price ranges, so you should be able to stay within your budget. You just have to look for the best value at the price you're willing to pay.

It's a good idea to get some advice from an expert, such as a wine merchant, a friend or relative who gives lots of parties, or a caterer or party planner. Then do some taste testing to find wines that appeal to you. The bonus of taking this task seriously is that tasting can be fun.

WINE FOR SPECIAL EVENTS

If your party is celebrating a major milestone—a notable birthday, an engagement, or a long partnership—sparkling wine can add the perfect touch. If price is no object, you've got lots of choice, among different US, French, and other producers.

But if you are keeping an eye on costs, one approach is to serve the sparkling wine just for the toast. That not only helps make the moment special, but it gives you more flexibility in what you spend, and the quality of wine you choose.

A SIMPLE BUDGET ITEM

Sticking to a wine budget is often easier than staying within your food budget. There are no hidden expenses, and you don't need to have anything extra on hand. It's really easy to overlook the cost of butter for the bread, cream for the coffee, and charcoal for the grill. But once you've paid for the wine, all you have to do is pour.

Serving Is Not Entertaining

Giving a party is not an endurance contest, but a time to spend with your guests.

Trying to serve wine on your own can be a daunting and even frustrating task when you're hosting a large party—whether it's a sit-down meal or a stand-up gathering. Most important, it takes concentration, which means spending less time with your guests. You can't handle introductions, open bottles, keep people's glasses full, and clear the empty glasses all at the same time, much less join in conversation.

One solution is to arrange for a bartender. You can ask a friend who is willing to take on the task, use someone on a friend's recommendation, or hire someone through a caterer. Or, if there's a college nearby, you might try calling the student employment office.

WHEN TO CALL FOR HELP
If you think you need help serving wine at a party, here are some things to consider:

Size. The larger the group, the more time opening bottles and pouring wine takes, so the more likely it is that you'll want some help.

Guest list. When the guests all know each other and they all know you, you may be comfortable letting them take care of themselves—or each other. But if the party is more formal, or if you're entertaining guests for the first time, you should consider getting help.

Physical space. If your party is spread out over several rooms, or is both indoors and outdoors, you may want to have more than one person serving wine to avoid the inevitable congestion of too many people in one place at one time.

HANDLING THE MECHANICS
Be sure to have the server (or servers) you're using arrive enough ahead of time so you can review where everything is and the order in which you want the wines served if you're offering more than one. That's the time to discuss what

the job entails—including clean up—and the amount you're paying.

Also be clear about what you expect. If you want the server to move about the room refilling glasses, say so. Or, you might prefer him or her to stay put and have your guests go to the serving area. What seems best may vary from party to party, depending on the space, number of people, and formality of the event.

You should demonstrate how much wine you want poured in a glass, or ask the server to pour a glass for you to be sure there's no overfilling. You'll be more comfortable if pouring is handled the way you'd do it yourself. And there won't be as much waste.

Organization is the key to a great party. If you figure out the flow, the way people will move through the party site, you can pinpoint the best places to put the wine and food tables.

—Ken Wolfe
Robbins Wolfe Eventeurs

BRING IN THE REINFORCEMENTS

If you're working with a caterer on the food, he or she can help you estimate the amount of wine you'll need and provide someone to serve. Some caterers will also offer a wine list you can choose from and arrange to have it ordered and delivered.

Taking advantage of this service may appeal to you, especially on a formal occasion or for the kind of party you haven't had much experience hosting. You might also benefit from professional advice on pairing the food and wine, much as you would working with a sommelier.

But if you prefer to choose and buy the wine yourself, it doesn't have to be a package deal. You'll probably have a wider choice and you may spend less since a caterer may mark up the cost per bottle somewhat to help cover costs.

PARTY GLASSES

Most parties require more wine glasses than you're likely to own, but that's no reason for not entertaining. You've got several options:

- Some wine shops keep a supply of glasses they lend to their customers for private parties. You may need to reserve them well ahead of time
- You can rent wine glasses from party suppliers, typically at modest cost. Some suppliers may offer glasses of different sizes and quality if you ask
- If you're working with a caterer, he or she can either supply the glasses or handle rental arrangements

- If you entertain frequently—and have enough storage space—you can buy several dozen glasses for relatively little, either at restaurant supply stores or department stores

You can always use plastic wine glasses, especially for informal parties and picnics. While plastic may offend some people, there's something to be said for being able to throw the glasses away at the end of a party. In fact, a big, crowded party is probably one place you don't want to use your best glasses. If the thought of one of them being accidentally dropped makes your blood run cold, why take the chance?

Telltale Tastes

Tasting wine in groups can be an education or just a social event.

Wine tastings can range from informal chats to intensive, high-level expert evaluations. Sitting on a patio on Saturday afternoon talking about why you like a bottle of wine you're sharing with friends is a wine tasting. So is a classroom where an instructor describes the characteristics of a group of similar wines and the students take small sips along with their notes. A gathering of wine professionals who are evaluating the most recent vintage of a particular varietal is also a wine tasting.

In fact, a wine tasting can be almost any situation where you pay attention to the wine you're drinking, discuss its flavor and bouquet, compare it to other wines, and describe your reaction to it.

PUBLIC DOMAIN

Everyone is welcome at many wine tastings—provided you're at least 21—including those offered by local wine shops and restaurants, those arranged as part of fund-raising events, or those given at local colleges, continuing education programs, or community centers. In fact, these tastings are designed specifically to help you learn more about wine and make drinking it more fun.

If you live in an area where it's hard to find an organized tasting—in some places, for example, a wine-shop tasting may violate local laws—you can check out a number of wine websites to find an online tasting group to share your reactions and ideas with.

AT THE WINE SHOP

In many parts of the country, wine retailers schedule regular tastings for their customers and

BYOB

You and your friends can plan your own wine tastings, and have the added benefit of enjoying each other's company. It doesn't matter if these tastings are completely spontaneous or follow a more regular schedule—the second Saturday of every month, or the third Tuesday of every other month, or whatever works.

One way to distinguish a wine-tasting evening from your other get-togethers—if that's what you want to do—is to organize each evening around a theme.

Tonight's Wine

Pick a varietal
You could taste only cabernet sauvignon, or only sauvignon blanc, or another varietal or blend. You could choose wines from the US or South America or Australia, or bottles from each region.

Pick a country
You might focus on French or Italian wine, choosing wines from one region within the country or from several.

Our extraordinary long family tradition plays an important role in terms of love and passion for the product. It has been transferred from generation to generation over the last six centuries. My duty and challenge is to be able to transfer this cultural value to the future generations.

—*Piero Antinori*
Antinori

prospective customers. If the place where you shop doesn't do it, ask. A little encouragement may spur the owner to action.

Wine-shop tastings can be organized in different ways. Some focus on current releases and may sell wines that are being featured at reduced prices on the day (or evening) of the tasting. Some tastings are organized to showcase the wines of a particular producer or to explore a particular varietal. Sometimes a winemaker or other wine industry representative is part of the program.

Wine-shop tastings are usually informal, low-keyed events, providing a chance to taste a variety of types and styles of wines in different price categories. They also give you a chance to meet other people who share your interest in wine in an atmosphere that encourages you to talk about your reactions to what you're drinking or just listen to what others are saying.

WHO/WHERE

A wine tasting group can be any size—from three to a dozen or more people—and any mix of ages, interests, experience, and backgrounds. You can have your wine tastings at home or in an agreeable restaurant. In that case, you may want to work out an arrangement with the owner that lets you bring some or even all of the wines.

The more people at the tasting, the more wines you can taste. If you figure six to eight glasses per bottle with a meal, you can double the number if you're serving tasting portions.

PRACTICAL CONSIDERATIONS

In addition to the convivial appeal of social wine tastings, there are some practical advantages:

One is price. Since you're sharing the cost, you can afford to buy more wine or more expensive wine than an individual budget may bear.

Another is variety. Sharing makes it practical to taste several wines. Otherwise you face the dilemma of limiting your selection or having to figure out what to do with a number of partly finished bottles.

A third advantage is research. If several of you share responsibility for choosing the wines and keeping your (collective) eyes out for new ideas, you can cover a lot more ground.

Tasting

Pick a date
You might choose several reds from 1995, or taste a number of different whites from 1997.

Pick a surprise
One evening you might taste only varietals or blends you'd never tried before.

Pick a price
One evening you might decide, quite arbitrarily, to drink only wines that cost less than $10 a bottle, or less than $15 a bottle, or whatever price you choose. Or you might try bottles of the same varietal at different price ranges.

123

The Taste Test

Some tastings are designed to produce winners.

While a wine doesn't need a blue ribbon or a gold star for you to enjoy drinking it, wines are being evaluated and rated all the time.

astounding how wrong even the most experienced tasters can be on occasion. On the other hand, blind tastings are the most reliable way to form an opinion unclouded by what you think you like or don't like.

In an **open** tasting, on the other hand, all the participants know what the wines are before they take a sip. Wine appreciation courses, wine shop tastings, and most social events tend to be open tastings.

BLIND VS. OPEN

TASTING BLIND

In a **blind** wine tasting, participants aren't told what they're drinking. Typically, the wine bottle is covered (usually with a bag or wrapping), or the wine is decanted, or the glasses are poured away from the table and arranged in a particular order. Once the tasters have decided what they think about each wine and ranked it in relation to the others in the tasting, the wines are identified.

In some blind tastings, the group is told the varietal, the origin, or the vintage to help them evaluate the wine within a particular context. But other tastings are blinder than that. In a double blind tasting, the tasters aren't told anything at all: not the varietal or blend, the origin, or the vintage.

As anyone who has ever been part of a blind tasting will tell you, it's

1996

Château de Hautier

MERLOT

A blind tasting in Paris in 1976 put the US on the world's wine map. California chardonnays were judged superior to fine white Burgundies, and California cabernet sauvignons beat out fine red Bordeaux.

OTHER WAYS TO TASTE

When you taste a number of wines of the same varietal or type from the same vintage, you're doing what's known as a **horizontal** tasting. In a **vertical** tasting, on the other hand, you taste several vintages, usually consecutive ones, typically of the same wine produced by the same winery.

For example, a horizontal cabernet sauvignon tasting might feature half a dozen bottles of that varietal produced in 1995. But a vertical tasting might include six bottles of the same wine produced each year from 1989 to 1994.

A horizontal tasting can help you see the similarities and differences in wines produced in different locations and by different winemakers. Chances are you'll prefer some wines to others, and tasting them together can help you figure out why.

A vertical tasting lets you experience how a wine's style develops as it ages and can demonstrate whether the style has been consistent or not over the years. It can also show how vintage variations can affect consistency.

You can also do a hybrid tasting, choosing bottles of the same type of wine produced by different wineries over a period of several years. Because of differences in vineyard locations and winemaking styles, this approach doesn't provide the definitive comparisons of a true vertical tasting. But it can give you a general impression of the varietal in various vintages.

TWO TASTING DIRECTIONS

Cabernet Sauvignon From Various Wineries

'95 CAB '95 Cab '95 CAB '95 Cab '95 CAB '95 CAB

HORIZONTAL VS. VERTICAL

SERIOUS EVALUATIONS

Wine associations, community groups, and even county fairs host wine tastings to evaluate, discuss, and award medals or other marks of distinction to certain wines. These tastings are usually chaired by a wine critic or educator and involve tasters with experience in this type of event, though they're not necessarily professionals. In most cases, the wines are served blind to counter any preconceived notions about the quality of certain brands, varietals, areas of origin, or vintages.

These evaluations often involve 30 to 80 tasters reviewing as many as 1,000 or more wines. Tasters are often divided into smaller groups of six to eight people, with each group tasting specific wines during the preliminary rounds. For example, one group of six to eight tasters might be responsible for evaluating 100 or more wines (obviously a situation that calls for spitting rather than swallowing) and identifying their favorites. In the final rounds, all the tasters retaste the finalists chosen by the groups, and select those to be singled out for honors.

Many wine journals and newsletters also conduct regular tastings to evaluate newly released as well as older wines. These tastings are done by smaller groups—often including wine writers, critics, and editors. Again, most wines—but not necessarily all—are tasted blind, and the ratings, recommendations, and opinions are featured in the sponsoring publications.

Cabernet Sauvignon From One Winery

1998

1997

1996

1995

1994

$\mathcal{E}$ ducating Your Palate

You can learn a lot when you drink in class.

Though wine—even Rhine wine—probably doesn't qualify as one of the three Rs, it's a favorite subject in both traditional and non-traditional academic settings. In fact, you can find a class where you can learn more about wine whether you're an absolute beginner or an experienced wine aficionado.

LEARNING BY TASTING

Tasting is a central theme in all wine classes. At the beginner level, the instructor may cover several types of wine so you'll have a general introduction to the subject. In more advanced classes, you may concentrate in greater depth on certain regions, wineries, vintages, or styles.

In some introductory classes, instructors add ingredients to a jug wine to help you identify characteristic flavors and components more easily. For example, adding tartaric acid demonstrates what acidity means, adding sugar focuses on sweetness, adding glycerin helps illustrate silkiness, and adding tannin (usually from tea) helps illustrate its mouth-puckering effect. After tasting these concoctions, it's often easier for you to identify the flavors and components in wines where they appear naturally.

Whatever class you're taking, your homework is to keep tasting and experimenting. It's the best way to discover wines you enjoy. And it can be an incentive to put together a small study group so you and your classmates can continue to taste and talk about wine together.

DEGREES OF LEARNING

Many colleges and universities offer an introduction to wine course that requires taking tastes as well as taking notes. These highly popular classes are often part of the regular curriculum and carry academic credit, though they may be limited to students who are at least 21.

Generally the course is an overview of the history of wine and winemaking, a survey of the wines produced in the major winemaking regions of the world, and the basic vocabulary you need to buy and discuss wine. Sometimes these courses are also offered during summer session or as part of an extension program, so you don't have to be a full-time student to enroll.

In more specialized environments, students can major in wine, or food and wine. Well-known programs include those offered by the Department of Viticulture and Enology at the University of California at Davis, at Cornell University's School of Hotel Administration, and at a range of culinary schools, including the flagship Culinary Institute of America (CIA).

If you're interested in taking a formal course, or a more advanced class, check to see if there's a program at a school near you. Or you might be able to find special courses or institutes, often a week or two long, that are open

A HANDY REFERENCE

If you want some help locating a class where you can learn more about wine, get in touch with the Society of Wine Educators. Their phone number is 202-347-5677. You can find them on the Internet at wine.gurus.com

Welcome to Wine Tasting 101
In this course you will learn:
- Choosing essentials
- How wine is made
- Vocabulary & pronunciation
- reading labels from around the globe
- How to pair food & wine

the mystery and mythology out of wine, the classes tend to be relaxed and unintimidating.

If you're an experienced wine drinker, there are courses that let you build on what you know, typically with other people who are interested in—and maybe passionate about—the same subject. You may find courses on collecting wines, on developing your tasting skills, on cooking with wine, or an array of other choices. And if there's a subject that interests you that hasn't been covered, you can probably find someone to offer it.

to the public. They may be advertised in wine or food magazines, in wine newsletters, and on wine websites.

SCHOOL FOR FUN

If you investigate, you'll probably be able to find wine appreciation classes offered by wine shops, wine societies, and individuals who enjoy sharing their love of wine with others. Some sessions are designed for people who have just started to appreciate wine, and others for people hungry (or thirsty) to learn more.

For the beginner, a major benefit is an introduction to the vocabulary of wine and the essentials of choosing and enjoying wine. That might include learning how wine is made, how to read the labels from the different wine growing regions around the world, how to pronounce a wine's or grape's name confidently, and how to pair wines with foods. Since the primary goal is to take

FOOD AND WINE

Restaurants may feature special wine-tastings, or food- and wine-tastings, organized around a particular events, varietals, or wine producers. If you want to know what it's like to drink sparkling wine throughout a meal, or have a different wine with every course, these are occasions to look for.

One experiment you might try, for example, is to taste each wine before you eat the food it accompanies, and then taste it again after you've taken a bite. You might find that a wine seems more mellow or more acidic than it did before, or that the flavor seems quite different.

You might even ask a restaurant to put together an event for a group you organize. You could give the chef and sommelier free rein (though you'd probably want to agree on a price range), or work out the menu and wine pairings ahead of time.

Select and Collect

Some people collect stamps or baseball cards or antique jewelry. Others collect wine.

You're not a stamp collector if you have a packet of stamps in your desk. Nor are you a jewelry collector if you store your grandfather's cufflinks in your drawer. So are you a wine collector if you have a bottle or two in the hall closet? Not exactly. But when you've started to accumulate a few bottles, and you're trying to figure out where to store the ones you want to buy, you're on the way. After all, it's the unusual person who wakes up one day and decides to be a collector. It's more likely to evolve as an avocation—or a passion.

There's no such thing as a typical wine collection. You can invest large amounts of money, and build an elaborate cellar with hundreds or even thousands of bottles of wine. But if you put away a dozen or so bottles that you look forward to drinking or that you want to open on a special occasion, that's a collection, too.

COLLECTING IS YOUR CALL

Probably the most obvious reason to collect wine is that you'll have a bottle to open and enjoy whenever you please. You won't have to plan ahead if you decide to serve wine with a spur-of-the-moment dinner, or if friends stop by for the evening. And if you start to collect different styles of wine, you'll have something that suits almost every occasion.

Specializing in a particular type of wine, such as cabernet sauvignon, or wine from a particular region, is another way to collect. In that case, your goal is more likely to be depth than breadth—many of one variety rather than many different varieties. Some collectors, for example, buy only rare or unusual wines.

BUY NOW, DRINK LATER

Another reason to buy ahead, which for many is what wine collecting is all about, is that many premium wines are produced in limited quantities. If you want to drink them, you often have to buy them when they're released. Chances are they won't be available later, or, if you can find them, they will be very expensive. Similarly, having a collection lets you stock up on wine you especially like when it's available at a good price.

Some collectors use a buy-and-hold strategy for wines that they expect to appreciate in quality and value. They either drink the wines when they reach their prime, or sell them at a profit. While investing in wine has risks, they can be balanced by the potential for significant financial return if, as with all investing, you know what you're doing.

SO WHAT'S A WINE FUTURE?

Buying wine futures means you pay now for wine that will be delivered at some point in the future, after the bottling and retail release. The upside is that if the vintage turns out to be an exceptional one, you will have paid less than the market price when the wine is released. The downside is that there are no guarantees that the wine will live up to the expectations you have for it.

HUMBLE BEGINNINGS

If you're just starting to collect wines, the most perplexing problem is deciding what to buy. Buying wines that you've tasted works well if you buy from a local merchant where you can go back for more, or if you visit a winery where you can taste a number of wines and then purchase what you like. If you have the opportunity to buy wine from a winemaker's mailing list, or you shop for wines on the Internet, tasting wine before buying it isn't always possible.

Ideally, you should buy to please yourself, and not try to keep up with the latest rage. On the other hand, new wines are being introduced all the time. If you make it a point to experiment at a tasting or by ordering something new in a restaurant, you might discover a new favorite.

You can seek advice and suggestions from other wine enthusiasts and pay attention to what you read or hear. But be sure to buy what you like. You don't want to use up valuable storage space or spend money on wines you don't really enjoy.

> You know you're a wine collector when you realize you're buying more wine to drink next year than to drink tonight.
>
> —*Robin Garr*
> *The Wine Lover's Page*
> *www.winelovers.com*

WORD OF MOUTH

If you're building a collection, you can learn a lot from other people who have collections, as well as from experts who write about famous collections and collectors.

Start by getting to know a wine retailer who is interested in you and your reasons for collecting wine. Ask your friends where they shop, or visit several different stores and talk to the owner or manager. Once you've established a relationship, you'll get tips on new wines as they come in and hear about special promotions or good prices.

Making Room for Wine

You'll be surprised how much wine you can store if you put your mind to it.

Enjoying wine isn't an equipment-intensive hobby, but figuring out how to store even a modest collection can be a real challenge.

CREATING THE RIGHT ENVIRONMENT

If you have an extra closet, or some space in your basement or garage, you might want to investigate the cost of fitting it out as a wine cellar with temperature and humidity controls. You can ask your wine merchant to recommend someone who specializes in that kind of remodeling or ask for references from other collectors. It may not be cheap to do the initial construction, and you'll have to add a racking system to hold the bottles.

Another solution to wine storage problems is to buy an enclosed unit that controls the temperature and humidity. These units are available in a broad range of sizes and styles, and at a variety of prices. Some of the smaller ones hold a case or two, and fit on a kitchen counter. Some of the larger ones may hold 700 bottles or more. Generally speaking, the only thing you have to decide is where to plug it in.

Or, you can buy a wooden racking system. They're also available in a variety of materials, designs, and storage capacities. Like the self-contained systems, some racking systems are decorative and others are strictly utilitarian. The greatest advantage is that they are significantly cheaper than the controlled-environment units. But you'll still have to deal with the issues of humidity and temperature if you plan to hold the wines for a period of time in an open storage area.

Another option is to store wine in the wooden boxes, cardboard cases, or styrofoam shipping

Styrofoam shipping box

boxes the bottles come in. Attractive they aren't. But they're functional and inexpensive. As an added plus, styrofoam is a good way to help keep the wine temperature more stable. But you should still use a closet where the temperature is constant if you can.

WHICH SIDE UP?

Wine keeps best when you store it horizontally, so that the liquid is in contact with the cork. That helps keep the cork moist and therefore tight in the bottle.

With a wine that produces sediment as it ages, that sediment will collect along the side that's facing down. If you keep the bottle horizontal when you take it out of the rack, keeping that side down, you don't risk redistributing the sediment just before serving, and you make decanting it or pouring it directly into the glass easier. If you're always careful to put bottles into the rack with the label facing up, you won't forget which side has been down.

To remember where the sediment is—
LABEL UP!

WHAT'S IN THE CELLAR?

As your collection grows, you'll probably need a system for keeping track of what you own and where it is in your storage area. After all, it can be frustrating to know you have the perfect bottle to pair with a meal if you can't put your hands on it.

If you're really methodical, you can devise a logical system that separates your collection into specific categories, by place of origin or vintage. Then at least you know on which shelves or in which boxes to look. Another approach is to keep a written or computerized record that you update each time you add to the collection or take a bottle out. It's the same approach restaurants use so they can keep their wine lists up to date and find the bottle a customer has ordered.

You can create your own recordkeeper with a loose-leaf notebook or database program, or you can buy a commercial software package or cellar book. There are several different ones available that you can customize to suit the information you want to include.

my cellar book

REMOTE CONTROLS

If you don't have enough space or the right conditions to store wines at home, you may be able to locate commercial wine storage facilities for long-term storage. They're basically private lockers that provide the right conditions, ideally in a convenient location and at a reasonable price. Your wine merchant or the sommelier at your favorite restaurant may be able to make a recommendation, or you can consult the yellow pages.

The only real disadvantage is that it's not as easy to pick out a bottle on the spur of the moment. So keep some at home as well.

Environmental Controls

Wines are happiest when temperature and humidity are consistent.

You can improve the chances that the wine you buy will be in good shape when you drink it if you're careful about the place where you store it. You can start by asking yourself these questions:

• Is the temperature relatively constant year around and can it be controlled?

• Is the amount of light limited?

• Is the space free from vibrations from appliances or heavy traffic?

• Is the humidity about right and is it relatively constant?

TAKING THE LOCAL TEMPERATURE

There are ideal storage conditions for a wine collection—a quiet, dark space that's a constant 55° Fahrenheit (13° Celsius). That's the natural temperature of most European wine caves. And that temperature is what winemakers and collectors throughout the world strive to achieve in their storage spaces.

That doesn't mean wine can't be stored safely at other temperatures. In fact, anywhere between 52° and 59° Fahrenheit is probably close enough. And wine that you're likely to drink within a few months after buying it can be stored without harm at somewhat warmer temperatures for that period of time.

AGING BY DEGREES

The pace at which wine ages, or develops its full flavor and bouquet, depends in large part on the temperature at which it's stored.

A wine stored at 65° Fahrenheit will mature faster than one stored at 55°. A wine stored at 45° will mature more slowly and may not develop at all, even if you store it for an extended period at that temperature. That's one of the reasons you can't simply press an old refrigerator into service for storing wine. It's much too cold.

The best temperature for a wine cellar is 55°F. But anywhere between 52° and 59° is fine.

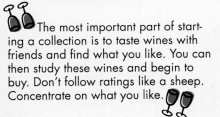

The most important part of starting a collection is to taste wines with friends and find what you like. You can then study these wines and begin to buy. Don't follow ratings like a sheep. Concentrate on what you like.

—Dr. Bipin Desai
Wine collector

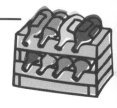

HUMIDITY YOU CAN STAND

When the humidity level in your storage area is at the right level—about 70%—corks can do their job of protecting the wine from air. But if the room is too dry, corks may get dry and shrink slightly. That lets air into the bottle, so the wine will age more quickly and may even oxidize and spoil.

Streaks of wine staining the capsule, bottle, or label are tell-tale evidence of dryness because the wine can leak only if the cork has shrunk or was defective to begin with. And remember, if there's not enough humidity in the room, the cork can dry out even if you've been careful to store the bottle on its side to keep the cork moist from the inside.

On the other hand, if your storage space gets too damp, the moisture may loosen the labels, which can make it hard to know what you're drinking. Airborne molds may also grow on the bottle or under the capsule, although that doesn't happen often, and it doesn't affect the quality of the wine.

In addition, most experts agree it's more important to keep the temperature in your storage space constant—as long as it's not really hot or really cold—than it is to keep the temperature at 55°. The more constant the conditions are outside the bottle, the more smoothly the aging process progresses. But if the temperature fluctuates dramatically, the chemical reactions that are part of aging speed up and slow down in response to the changes. Such erratic movement disrupts the reactions and may mean the wines don't age as gracefully as they could have under more favorable conditions. That means that they can't live up to their full potential.

The humidity in a wine cellar should be at least 70%.

A DELICATE BALANCE

You can track the humidity in a storage area using a **hygrometer**, which you can buy in hardware stores, some wine shops, and from mail order and Internet catalogs that feature wine products. Some hygrometers are paired with thermometers, so they measure temperature as well.

A Bid for Wine

Wine auctions are a great source for wines.

If you can't find a particular wine in a retail store, you might try buying one or more bottles at auction. In fact, an auction may be your only source for a rare or highly regarded wine—a wine from an older vintage, or a vertical collection, for example.

Once a wine has been released for sale, and there are no more bottles available from the winery, people who own the wine may be interested in selling it. In fact, they may have bought a number of bottles with the intention of selling them at a profit.

An auction can make it happen.

competing against each other until no bidder will offer a higher price. The sale is completed on the spot at the highest price offered.

While the largest and most successful commercial auctions are held in California, New York, and Illinois, you can often bid on items by phone, fax, or on the Internet while the auction is in progress. Or you can submit written bids by mail before the auction begins.

Newer **online auctions** operate a bit differently, since they take place in virtual, rather than real, space. That gives more buyers greater access to the

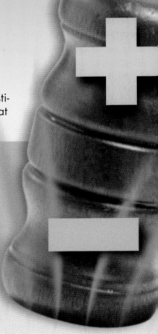

AUCTION PROS AND CONS
There are advantages and some disadvantages in buying wine at an auction.

Advantages
+ Auctions may be the only way to buy wine no longer available in the retail market, especially older vintages and hard-to-find bottles.
+ While auction prices are often dictated by sophisticated bidders and collectors, you can also find great bargains, with prices below the retail market price.

Disadvantages
– The wines being auctioned may not have been stored carefully. If there's a problem, older vintages in particular may not be in good condition. All reputable commercial auction houses, web sites, and well-established charity auctions take extraordinary measures to minimize this potential problem. But there is always a risk.
– Expert wine collectors from around the world are willing to buy unusual and hard-to-find lots at virtually any price. That can also drive up the prices of similar lots.

GOING, GOING, GONE
There are three basic types of wine auctions.

Commercial auctions are organized by a national auction house like Christie's or Sotheby's or by local auction companies. They're held at a specific time and place, with bidders

auction and lets bidders everywhere participate on their own schedule and at their own pace. Typically, these auctions are held over a period of days or weeks, with participants following the action on their computers and submitting higher offers, if they choose, to stay in the bidding. Some sites will notify

> Online auctions have single-handedly democratized the world of fine and rare wines. Now absolutely anybody can participate, no matter where they are or who they know or don't know.
>
> *—Ursula Hermancinski*
> *Winebid.com*

Like commercial auctions, they may offer absentee bidding systems, although the setup varies with each event.

AUCTION STRATEGIES

With wine auctions, as with other auctions, you need to know what you are bidding on, and what you are willing to pay for a particular lot, in order to take advantage of the sometimes unusual items that come up for sale. Then you need discipline to stick to your resolve. Emotion and desire can often take over, and you can end up paying prices you know are excessive.

You must also consider any added expense of shipping, packing and handling, as well as the commission or buyer's premium (usually 10% to 15%) that might be added to the sale price at an online or commercial auction. That won't be an issue at a charity auction.

In addition, you need to check your state's laws to see if there are any restrictions on having wine you purchase shipped to you. The organizers or sponsors should know the answer. Online auction sites, for example, list the states that do not permit them to ship your purchases to an address in those states.

you by email if another bidder offers a higher price.

When the auction ends, the highest bidder has bought the wine. Purchases are guaranteed with a credit card, although you usually must send a check and a written confirmation to have the wine shipped to you.

Charity wine auctions, which are staged as fundraising events for charitable organizations, are also a relatively new phenomenon. Auctions like these raise significant amounts of money in many cities across the country and give buyers an opportunity to accomplish two goals—to buy wine that may not be otherwise available and to benefit the charity.

The auctions, which are often conducted by a well-known auctioneer, feature wines that donors have contributed. Donors are often happy to participate since they know their wines are going to a worthy cause and that the buyers will enjoy their purchases.

> Buying at auction is a great way to obtain old and rare vintages of wine, and it's lots of fun. But you should research the prices at which the wines you're interested in have sold recently. Then set a limit and stick to it.
>
> *—Ann Colgin*
> *Consultant, Sotheby's Wine*
> *Department*

LOT # 26B
VERY RARE

Wine Vacations

The best way to get a real feel for winemaking is to visit the wine country.

Many of the best-known winemaking regions of the world are also wonderful vacation destinations. Not only are they physically beautiful, but they're often surprisingly easy to get to. And while they can be crowded at the height of the vacation season, most welcome visitors all year around.

You can plan a trip on your own. There's no shortage of travel guides for the best known areas, such as the Napa and Sonoma Valleys in California, the Champagne, Burgundy, and Bordeaux regions of France, Tuscany and Piedmont in Italy, the Hunter and Yarra Valleys of Australia or the Rheingau in Germany. Or you can join one of the hundreds of organized wine-country tours that are offered every year to fit almost every taste and pocketbook.

You can also expand your horizons by visiting wineries closer to home. You may be astonished to discover there are some fascinating ones within a few hours drive from almost anywhere.

WINERY TOURS

You can take regularly scheduled winery tours that give you an overview of the entire winemaking process from the vineyards to aging cellars, both in the US and in other winegrowing regions.

In California's many wine areas, for example, many of the wineries welcome visitors without reservations, but you'll find you need one at others. Often a phone call close to the time you want to visit is fine, but if you want to visit several places on a relatively tight schedule, it pays to make appointments well in advance. And if you're particularly interested in some phase of the operation, or if you want to visit a favorite winery that's not generally open to the public, making arrangements ahead is often essential. A letter or a phone call should do the trick.

> Fate brought me to the wine country and the fabled French Laundry. The region's nearly endless supply of fresh ingredients and our guests' boundless enthusiasm has let me continue to evolve the style of cuisine I have been developing throughout my career.
>
> —*Thomas Keller*
> *The French Laundry*

If you visit a number of wineries, you'll discover that while basic winemaking is essentially the same, each winery uses slightly different techniques, and that every tour guide has a unique take on the industry. You'll find, too, that size makes a huge difference in the way an operation is run, as does the market the producer is trying to reach. If you visit both historic and modern wineries, you'll also realize how much the winemaking process has remained the same over the years, despite the obvious impact of technology.

THE TASTING ROOM

The tasting room is the last stop on most winery tours. There you can sample the wines that have been released most recently. Or, by making arrangements ahead of time, you can sometimes schedule a more extensive tasting. While many tastings are free, don't be surprised if you're asked to pay a few dollars at others.

If you taste a wine you like, you may want to buy several bottles or a case, especially since many smaller wineries don't have a huge distribution and can be hard to find at home. You may also ask about being included on the winery's mailing list so you'll have an opportunity to buy wines as they are released. But check with the staff about whether they can legally ship the wine to your home state, since laws vary. The alternative is to ask for a list of retailers or distributors in your home area who carry the wines.

WINE FOR ALL SEASONS

Deciding when you want to visit can make a big difference in the cost and the ease of getting reservations in local hotels and restaurants. Summer and harvest time, typically September and October in the northern hemisphere and March and April below the equator, are by far the most popular times for visitors. If you plan to visit during those times, make sure you book early and are prepared for the crowds.

Prices are generally lower in the winter, spring, and later fall, and you may get more personal attention from winemakers and tour guides when they're not overrun with other guests. That's true, as well, with restaurant reservations and hotel rooms—especially the best-known and most beautiful spots. Any time of year, though, a wine country vacation is a special treat.

I JUST WENT TO WINE COUNTRY

WINE COUNTRY OR BUST

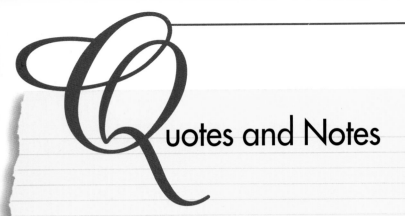

Quotes and Notes

Producer:
Name of Wine:
Vintage:
Appearance:

Nose:

Flavor:

Texture:

Comments:

Producer:
Name of Wine:
Vintage:
Appearance:

Nose:

Flavor:

Texture:

Comments:

Chile has reigned as the king of South American wines, especially in quality at lower prices. But Argentina is certainly the crown prince in waiting for the more premium wines.

—Nick Ramkowsky
Vine Connections

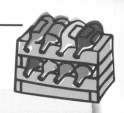

Producer:
Name of Wine:
Vintage:
Appearance:

Nose:

Flavor:

Texture:

Comments:

Producer:
Name of Wine:
Vintage:
Appearance:

Nose:

Flavor:

Texture:

Comments:

BOOKS FROM LIGHTBULB PRESS

Lightbulb Press books are available in bookstores everywhere. Visit us on the World Wide Web at www.lightbulbpress.com. Contact us at (917) 256-4900 for information on quantity discounts.

THE WALL STREET JOURNAL GUIDE TO UNDERSTANDING MONEY & INVESTING

by Kenneth M. Morris and Virginia B. Morris

The ideal introduction to investing—and the perfect reference for the experienced investor. Over 1,000,000 copies sold.

Stocks • Bonds • Mutual Funds • Indexes • Risk/Return • Tracking Performance • Evaluating Companies • Investing Online

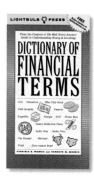

DICTIONARY OF FINANCIAL TERMS

by Virginia B. Morris and Kenneth M. Morris

The most important investing terms people hear and read every day—explained in language everyone can understand. Free online updates at www.lightbulbpress.com.

Hundreds of Definitions • Financial Acronyms • The Difference between Markets and Exchanges • Reading a Stock Ticker • Tracking the Markets

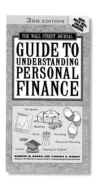

THE WALL STREET JOURNAL GUIDE TO UNDERSTANDING PERSONAL FINANCE

by Kenneth M. Morris and Virginia B. Morris

The basics of personal finance—and the pitfalls to avoid along the way in everyday financial life.

Bank Accounts • Credit Cards • Mortgages • Financial Planning • College Education • Investing • Online Banking • Taxes • Planning for Retirement

A WOMAN'S GUIDE TO INVESTING

by Virginia B. Morris and Kenneth M. Morris
Introduction by Bridget A. Macaskill

The essential information—and inspiration—women of all ages need to manage their financial lives.

Setting Financial Goals • Making Smart Investment Decisions • Choosing a Financial Advisor • Investing with and without a Partner • Dealing with the Expected and Unexpected

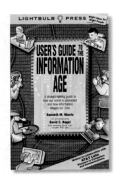

USER'S GUIDE TO THE INFORMATION AGE

by Kenneth M. Morris
Introduction by David C. Nagel

The bits and bytes behind the technologies that are changing everyday life in the 21st century.

Using Computers • Surfing the Internet • Connecting with Cell Phones • Enjoying Smart Appliances • Managing Online Accounts • Living in the Electronic Age

CREATING RETIREMENT INCOME

by Virginia B. Morris
Introduction by Mark J. Mackey

An in-depth look at building and managing retirement income—with a special focus on the role annuities play in an overall retirement plan.

Asset Accumulation • Income Streams • Withdrawal Options • Rollovers • Diversified Portfolios • Variable Annuities

THE WALL STREET JOURNAL GUIDE TO PLANNING YOUR FINANCIAL FUTURE

by Kenneth M. Morris, Alan M. Siegel
and Virginia B. Morris

An all-inclusive guide to retiring in comfort, including the information you need to make smart long-term decisions.

Investment Strategies • Salary Reduction Plans • Social Security • Insurance • Pension Plans • Long-term Care • Estate Planning

THE WALL STREET JOURNAL GUIDE TO UNDERSTANDING MONEY & INVESTING IN ASIA

by Kenneth M. Morris, Alan M. Siegel
and Beverly Larson

A comprehensive overview of financial markets in the Asian-Pacific region and beyond.

Stocks • Bonds • Mutual Funds • Indexes • Risk/Return • Tracking Performance • Changing Currency Values